The
Admiral

The Admiral

the
David Robinson
Story

**Gregg Lewis
and Deborah Shaw Lewis**

ZONDER**kidz**

ZONDERVAN.com/
AUTHOR**TRACKER**
follow your favorite authors

ZONDERKIDZ

The Admiral: The David Robinson Story
Copyright © 2002, 2012 by Gregg and Deborah Shaw Lewis

This title is also available as a Zondervan ebook.
Visit www.zondervan.com/ebooks

Requests for information should be addressed to:

Zonderkidz, 5300 Patterson Ave., SE, Grand Rapids, Michigan 49530

Library of Congress Cataloging-in-Publication Data

Lewis, Gregg, 1951
    The admiral : the David Robinson story / Gregg Lewis.
        p. cm.   (Zonderkidz biography)
      ISBN 978-0-310-72520-6
      1. Robinson, David, 1965   Juvenile literature. 2. Basketball players—United
States--Biography—Juvenile literature. 3. Christian athletes—United
States—Biography. I. Title.
GV884.R615L47 2012
796.323092—dc23
    [B]   2001017679

Editor: Kim Childress
Cover design: Kris Nelson
Interior design: Ben Fetterley
Interior composition: Greg Johnson/Textbook Perfect

Printed in the United States of America

12 13 14 15 16 17 /DCI/ 21 20 19 18 17 16 15 14 13 12 11 10 9 8 7 6 5 4 3 2 1

Table of Contents

Chapter 1

More Than a Celebrity

Imagine looking up at a man who stands seven-feet, one-inch tall—a Hall-of-Fame basketball player, one of only four players in history ever to score over 70 points in an NBA game. He played on three Olympic basketball teams. He scored 20,790 points and had 10,497 rebounds in his professional career and was chosen as an NBA All-Star ten times.

And that man stands looking right at you in front of your friends, your family, and says:

"You have the ability to accomplish great things. Nothing will stand in your way. There is nothing for you to be afraid of.

"You have everything in front of you, every hope, every possibility. I expect you to become a leader, a citizen for this country. You have support. You are well prepared to take this next step. Understand that as you go along someone will always be there to help lift you up to the next level.

"And the Lord will always watch over your shoulder as you take your next step, preparing the way for you, so that you might have good success.

"I want you to walk in that power that the Lord gives you."

In May of 2011, the sixth graders at The Carver Academy (TCA) in San Antonio, Texas, did not have to imagine that scene. They heard David Robinson tell them those things the day they graduated from TCA.

Why was a world-famous basketball star like David Robinson talking to sixth graders at a school that had 120 students? Because it was all part of a dream. His dream. A very real dream he believed in so much that he had already invested more than a decade and $10 million of his own resources to see it come true.

Now imagine that same man—one of the greatest basketball players in history, a gifted athlete who won piles of trophies and awards, earned a fortune, and became famous around the world for spending his life playing a game—decided to go back to school to learn how to do a better job in a new career. Why?

He already had a first-class college degree in mathematics and computer science from the United States Naval Academy. His three teenage sons would soon be making their own college decisions. He was busy with The Carver Academy. Now a successful business man, he partnered with large corporations and advised

David Robinson stands well above his colleagues at seven feet tall as he delivers his message of encouragement.

rich and famous celebrities on how to positively impact needy communities and people by using their fame and fortune for good. Another company he started owns and manages millions of dollars of commercial real estate—office buildings, hotels, and more.

So why would someone with all that experience and success ever think he needed to go back to school to learn anything else? For the same reason he would speak at a sixth-grade graduation. Because of his convictions and personal belief in the importance of education and learning—whoever you are and wherever you are in life.

Once again imagine that man—David Robinson, basketball legend, successful businessman—standing behind the counter of a concession stand at a high school ball game. He needs to bend over a little—okay maybe a LOT—to talk to the customers.

Many people just order snacks. Since David is someone everyone in San Antonio recognizes wherever he goes, people are so surprised to "encounter" him that some stammer out their orders. Others simply stand and stare. A few ask if he'll sign their program, a crumpled scrap of paper pulled out of a pocket, their popcorn box, or whatever else they have on hand.

David Robinson just smiles as he takes their money, makes change, and hands out soft drinks, peanuts, candy bars, and such. Along with the occasional autograph.

Why does someone like David Robinson work in a high school concession stand? Because it's the high school his sons attend. And volunteering is what parents do. This too is who he is—a parent and not just a celebrity.

Sports Illustrated featured David on a cover in April, 1996, to accompany their article about his "glowing" attributes on and off the court.

David's example on and off the basketball court has inspired so many people over the years that *Sports Illustrated* ran a feature story about him in 1996 with a glowing, soft-focus cover photo titled "Saint David."

He's quick to say he's not a saint. Yet David Robinson does have an unusual and impressive story—one that neither begins nor ends with a sixth-grade graduation at The Carver Academy, working a high school concession stand, or going back to school to learn how to do a better job in a new career. Yet these are three recent and telling stops on one man's remarkable life journey ...

Chapter 2

A Terrible Accident

One morning in February 1966, Freda Robinson drove her husband, Ambrose, to work. An expert in sonar— a type of radar that scans things under water—Mr. Robinson was headed for South Africa aboard the U.S.S. Van Voorhis.

In the car with them were their children, two-year-old Kim and six-month-old David. Mrs. Robinson knew her husband would be gone for some time, so she had decided that she and the children would visit her sister in Rye Beach, New Hampshire, for the next several days.

The Robinsons lived in Newport, Rhode Island, only a two hour drive from Rye Beach. Ordinarily such a short trip would be no problem. But on this particular day, an ice storm was predicted.

Mr. Robinson was concerned about the approaching bad weather and urged his wife not to make the trip to

New Hampshire. But once she dropped off her husband at the ship, she searched the sky and decided the weather didn't look that bad. So she packed some clothes for herself and the kids and left for New Hampshire.

The drive turned out to be uneventful, and the Robinson family had a good time visiting with Freda's sister Jessie, her husband, Mitch, and their six children. But two days after they arrived, the ice storm finally came. The storm was so bad that only emergency vehicles were allowed on the road.

Mrs. Robinson got up that morning, took David out of his crib, and laid him on her bed. She left him there while she went into the kitchen to heat his bottle. While she waited for the bottle to get warm, she talked to her sister Jessie.

David's mother noticed that he had stopped crying, but she assumed he had fallen back asleep and kept visiting with Jessie.

When David's mother walked back into the room and did not see David on the bed, she quickly searched the floor, believing that he must have fallen off the bed. But she was not able to find him.

Mrs. Robinson's mind was swimming. Maybe her brother-in-law Mitch had picked up the baby? Running to the door of his room, she called out, "Mitch, do you have David?"

"No," he answered.

"Don't kid me," David's mother told him.

Mitch came out in his bathrobe and repeated, "I don't have him, Freda."

Now Mrs. Robinson was near panic. "Well, where is he?" She ran into the living room and asked the other children, "Is David here?"

"No, ma'am," they answered.

She ran back into the bedroom and looked again: beside the bed, under the bed, on the bed. Suddenly she saw the top of his head. He had fallen between the bed and the wall and was jammed between the two. He was just hanging there, his face tightly pressed into the mattress.

Grabbing him up, Mrs. Robinson noted that he had turned blue. As a nurse she knew that babies turn blue when they don't get enough oxygen. She was standing there crying loudly and pacing when her sister Jessie ran into the room.

"Stop it!" Jessie told her sister. "He will be dead if you don't give him CPR."

"I can't," David's mother sobbed. "I've never done CPR on a human. I've only done it on a mannequin."

"If you don't want him to die, you had better try," Jessie urged her.

Mrs. Robinson laid baby David down on the mattress and started the CPR that she had been trained to do. And she began to pray—loudly. Freda had always believed that God answers prayers. So she cried, "Lord, please don't let my baby die!"

Mrs. Robinson put her fingers into David's mouth, sweeping it to see if he had anything blocking his airway. He didn't. She put her ear against his chest and listened but could not hear him breathing. So she leaned over, tipped his head back, and breathed into his mouth and nose. She paused for three seconds and then blew air into his mouth again. David still wasn't breathing.

Mrs. Robinson blew another small breath into David's lungs, then paused three seconds and blew again.

She saw his little chest rise.

Jessie was watching, too. "It looks like he's breathing," she exclaimed.

Mrs. Robinson picked David up and saw his eyes roll back in his head. She thought he was about to go into convulsions. So she ran out of the bedroom, through the kitchen, and into the garage. She knew the cold air in the garage would shock him. And it worked! David's eyes stopped rolling, and he began to cry.

Mitch called for an ambulance, but with the roads in such bad shape from the ice storm, the emergency crew took longer than usual to get to the house. While they waited, David's mother wrapped him in blankets and tried to warm him up.

Finally, the emergency crew arrived. When they saw David, he was no longer blue. In fact, he looked fine to them. He was just cold.

They took him to the hospital where he was put in an isolette to help get his temperature back to normal. Still Mrs. Robinson worried. She was a nurse, so she knew a person can go without oxygen for only four to six minutes. After that, brain damage occurs.

When the doctors asked Mrs. Robinson how long David had been blue, she couldn't tell them. She wasn't sure how long she had been in the kitchen talking and laughing with her sister Jessie. And she had no idea how long it had taken David to scoot across the bed, fall down between the mattress and the wall, and get jammed so tight that he couldn't breath.

She thought she must have been out of the room at least five minutes, maybe several minutes longer. She hoped David had not been in distress that long. But there was no way to know for sure, so there was no way for the doctors to tell if—or how much—brain damage might have occurred.

"I'll have to wait until he starts learning and talking?" David's mother asked the doctor.

"That's about the size of it," he responded.

Now Mrs. Robinson had two things to worry about. How would they cope if David had indeed suffered brain damage, and how would she tell her husband, especially since he had asked her not to go to New Hampshire in the first place?

Because her husband was at sea, Mrs. Robinson couldn't telephone him. She had to let him know what happened in a letter.

Two days later, Jessie asked Freda to drive her to a local shopping center. The roads were still icy, but Freda agreed. In the 1960s, cars were not equipped with seat belts, and baby car seats had not yet been invented. His mother laid David down on the seat beside her in the car.

On the way to the shopping center, another driver lost control of her car on the ice and slid into the Robinson's car, hitting on David's side of the vehicle. David was not hurt. But Freda then had to write her husband another letter, describing yet another near tragedy that would not have happened if she had stayed home as he had asked her to. Ambrose was particular about the car, and she hated to have to tell him it had been so badly damaged.

Finally, Freda's husband got the letters and was able to call home. "Are you all right?" he asked. "Is David hurt? Did Jessie get hurt?"

Freda explained that the only casualty was the car. Ambrose was relieved to hear that his family was safe. He did not scold her for going to her sister's house. Mrs. Robinson was happy that her husband was more concerned about his family than the car. She felt bad enough as it was.

Her husband's reaction was one less thing to worry about, but Mrs. Robinson still had to face a more daunting concern. How long had David been without oxygen? Had he suffered brain damage while he hung trapped between the wall and the mattress that icy morning?

Three years is a long time to worry about something that important. But that is how long the Robinsons had to wait for their answers.

Chapter 3

Early Reader

Freda Hayes had met Ambrose Robinson at church one Sunday. He was in the Navy, stationed in Rhode Island. Freda was in nursing school in New Hampshire. She wanted to finish school and wasn't interested in getting serious about a boyfriend.

Since Ambrose was engaged to another woman, Freda thought that it was safe to be friendly with him. After church that Sunday they talked for a while, and then Freda invited him to come to the house and meet her family.

Ambrose's naval duties kept him at sea for months at a time. But whenever he came home, he would visit New Hampshire to see Freda.

On one of his leaves, Ambrose showed up at the nursing home where Freda was working part time and asked if she could leave work and go out with him. It was a curious request, and Freda assured Ambrose that she could not leave. She had just begun her shift and would be on duty until 11:00 p.m. that evening. But Ambrose persisted, asking her to find someone else to work her shift.

Freda finally agreed to call two of her fellow nurse's aides. The first was a woman with small children who could not come in on short notice. The second was a friend named Helen. Freda often filled in for Helen so that she could do things with her husband. Yet Helen did not want to come into work that night.

"Let's call your boss and talk with her," Ambrose persisted.

Freda's supervisor, Mrs. Callahan, lived on the top floor of the nursing home, but Freda did not want to ask her boss for the evening off. Still Ambrose kept insisting.

So Freda called and Mrs. Callahan came downstairs. Freda introduced her to Ambrose who told Mrs. Callahan that he had been at sea for three months and desperately wanted to spend the evening with Freda.

"What is she to you?" Mrs. Callahan asked.

"She is my fiancé," he answered.

That was news to Freda!

Mrs. Callahan gave the go-ahead.

As Freda and Ambrose walked across a playground, heading from the nursing home to her house, Freda scolded him. "Why did you tell that woman a lie? We aren't engaged! You are going to get me fired. And I need this job!"

David Robinson enjoys taking in a game with mother Freda and father Ambrose.

"I didn't lie," he answered. "We are going to get married."

And less than three weeks later, Freda Hayes and Ambrose Robinson did get married. The following year, their daughter Kimberly was born. Two years after that, on August 6, 1965, Freda had their second child, David Maurice Robinson.

In 1966, several months after Mrs. Robinson's near-disastrous visit to her sister's house that wintry February weekend, the Navy transferred her husband to Key West, Florida. The family lived there until David was three years old. One day while the Robinsons were traveling on a highway near Key West, their questions about whether or not David had suffered brain damage were answered.

The speed limit was 55 miles per hour, but Mr. Robinson was driving about 60 miles per hour. Three-year-old David stood up in the back seat, looked over his father's shoulder, and announced, "Daddy, you're speeding!"

"Oh really?" his father protested.

David pointed to a speed limit sign along the side of the road and then to the dashboard. "The speed limit is 55," David said. "And you're going 60."

David's parents looked at each other. They were surprised and relieved! If their three-year-old son could read the road sign and understand the measurement on a speedometer, his brain was almost certainly functioning just fine.

Actually, the Robinsons had suspected the truth for some time. Every morning, Mrs. Robinson would call Kimberly and David in to watch *The Dr. Seuss Show*, a television program they enjoyed. They would pull up their chairs in front of the TV, and when the host of the show announced which Dr. Seuss book they would be reading that day, David and Kimberly would grab the right book and read along.

David had not yet begun school, so the Robinsons didn't know if he was reading the books or if he had memorized them. But David surely was showing a healthy interest in books and reading.

Mrs. Robinson liked reading to her children and had story time with them almost every night. She made a game of learning and reading. Their family had a chalk-board on which Mrs. Robinson and the children could write words and a bulletin board where they put up little notes. She also had a yardstick, which the children used for measuring. Even when their family traveled, they read road signs, license plates, and the names of the cars they passed as they drove down the road.

The weather was usually warm and nice in Key West, Florida. One of David's favorite activities was riding his toy tractor. Sitting on the black seat of that green tractor, David would pedal up and down the sidewalks around their apartment complex.

It was a pleasant place to live, but things were not easy for the Robinsons. David's mother worked long hours at the hospital, and his father was often at sea for as many as 250 days a year, leaving Mrs. Robinson to raise two small children by herself. When he was at home, Mr. Robinson often invited his Navy buddies to the house where they competed to see who could drink the most beer. Mrs. Robinson decided that she wanted a divorce.

She talked to Liz, a friend at work, who was divorced. "Divorce is no picnic!" Liz told her. "Your husband is a good provider. He loves you and your kids! Why do you want to get rid of him?"

"I'm tired," Freda told her. "I can't handle this anymore."

Liz tried to talk Freda out of the divorce. But when Freda insisted, Liz recommended a lawyer.

Freda called her parents and asked for money to help pay for the lawyer. But her parents liked Ambrose and didn't think Freda had enough reason to divorce him. So they refused to send her money to help her leave her husband.

Still, Freda called the attorney's office to make an appointment. But the lawyer couldn't see her for two weeks.

"I have to see him very soon!" Freda protested.

"Is it a matter of life and death?" the receptionist asked.

"Yes!" Freda answered, so the lawyer agreed to see her during his lunch break that same day.

He listened to her problems and then told her, "You and your husband just need to learn how to communicate."

So the lawyer wrote Ambrose a letter. The next Saturday, David's parents went to see the lawyer together. They took Kimberly and David with them.

When the lawyer saw Kimberly and David in the waiting room, he exclaimed, "What precious children!" And he had his secretary give them cookies while he talked to Mr. and Mrs. Robinson in his office.

"Do you want to save this marriage?" he asked Ambrose.

"By all means!" Ambrose answered.

"Do you want to save this marriage?" he asked Freda.

"I guess so," Freda told him.

The lawyer spent forty-five minutes talking to them about how to work through their problems. By the time they left that day, both Freda and Ambrose were determined to make their marriage work.

Chapter 4

The Human Calculator

When David Robinson was four years old, his family moved to Norfolk, Virginia. The state of Virginia at that time did not offer public kindergarten. Feeling that all children need to attend kindergarten, David's parents scrimped and saved the money to send him to a private kindergarten at a Lutheran church.

By the time he began first grade, David's family lived in military housing on the naval base in Norfolk. The teachers at his school soon discovered that David Robinson was a very bright little boy.

One day at the beginning of the school year, David's teacher gave the students a test. David did so well that the teacher thought there might have been a mistake. She gave David another test similar to the first, and again he did remarkably well. Amazed, the teacher spoke with the principal who placed David in a room near his office, away from the other children, and tested him one more time. David did even better on the last test than he had on the others.

Soon David's intelligence began to create problems in the classroom. He would finish his work faster than any of the other children and got everything right. But once he was finished, he would distract the other children who were still working.

The principal and teachers called Mr. and Mrs. Robinson in for a conference. Maybe David needed to be in second grade instead of first, they suggested. He was doing so well that the other students were beginning to feel as if they were behind.

His parents didn't want David to skip to second grade. They felt it was important for him to be treated like a normal kid, so they asked David's teachers to let him do some second-grade, maybe even third-grade, work when he finished his first-grade activities. That would keep him busy and learning, and he wouldn't have time to bother the other children. The plan worked well. David thrived on the advanced work, and he no longer had time to bother the other children.

When David's dad came home from work, he would often sit down and play his favorite pieces on the piano. He had studied piano for ten years while he was growing up and played the piano in church as a teenager. Freda had admired the way Ambrose would play the piano for her when they were dating. Ambrose found it relaxing after a long day at work, and David loved to climb on his father's lap while he played.

One evening when David was five years old, Mr. Robinson had been playing piano with David next to him. Then Ambrose got up and walked into another room. A few moments later he was surprised to hear a familiar tune. David's parents walked in to see David at the piano playing the same song his father had just been playing.

"David!" his father exclaimed. "How did you learn to play that song?"

"I just watched you play, Dad," David explained.

David's dad immediately recognized that the boy was unusually talented and decided he should begin to teach David about music. He got the sheet music that he had used as a boy and used it to teach David, who turned out to be a quick learner. David soon learned to read and play from written music and to compose songs of his own. One of the first songs David played was "Moonlight Sonata," a difficult classical piece.

Just one month before David's sixth birthday, his younger brother, Chuck, was born. When his parents brought Chuck home from the hospital, David seemed to think he was a neat new toy.

By the time David started second grade, he was chosen to participate in a new program for gifted children. One day a week he and other gifted children from all over town went to a magnet school to take classes that would challenge them. The classes were held in two trailers behind the school.

David liked the gifted program. Being around other really bright kids gave him a chance to work at being the

As a member of the U.S. Senior Men's National Team in 1992, David takes a break from playing in Barcelona, Spain, to exercise his saxophone skills.

best in a group of others who were the best. At last, he felt challenged.

When David was in third grade, he loved to go shopping with his mother. After making out a grocery list, she and David would walk across a little bridge to the store together.

David's mother called him her "human calculator." By the time they reached the checkout line, David had totaled in his head the prices of the grocery items they had chosen. He could tell his mother exactly how much their groceries would cost. If it was going to cost more money than his mother had to spend, David could tell her what she needed to put back on the shelf. And David also helped her figure out which items were the best buy.

Every day Kim and David came home from school tired and hungry. So their mom would let them eat a snack and rest a little before starting their homework. But Mrs. Robinson refused to let them go anywhere or do anything else until their homework was completed.

David often finished all his homework while he was at school. But his parents thought he needed to study anyway. His mother often gave him extra books to read or some higher level work to do in the afternoons.

When Kim and David had questions about their homework, their mom made them look up the answers. She knew they were more likely to remember the things that they looked up for themselves.

Sometimes when Kim or David didn't have anything to do, their dad would point to a page in the dictionary and say, "Learn as many of these words as you can." Then he would come back later and quiz them. He thought of himself as one of their teachers. He loved to watch them learn.

David and Kim liked to learn new words to use in the many games they played together as a family, like Scrabble.

David loved to read. One Saturday when he was in the fifth grade, he talked his mother into taking him to a bookstore. David loved science fiction, and his mother had promised to buy him a particular book he had been wanting.

"Mom, here's the one I want. And look! They have all five books in the series. Can we buy all of them?" David asked.

"No," his mother told him. "I promised to buy you one book."

But David continued to pester her for the entire series, and she finally relented. After all, she thought, you can never spoil a child with too many books.

David didn't read all the time. He also liked to play. The Robinson family went fishing and bowling together. They also played golf, baseball, football, basketball, tennis, and Ping-Pong together.

When Mr. Robinson was not at sea, he tried to make the most of the time he had with his children. After teaching them how to play a new game, he would play with his kids for hours.

David's dad also liked to watch sports on television with his children. During the broadcasts, they would discuss the rules and why things were happening the way they were. They also talked about the games afterward, so Kim, David, and Chuck knew a lot about sports even before they played them.

While they lived in Virginia Beach, David's dad taught bowling to nine and ten year olds. He taught David how to hit a baseball both right and left handed. He also served as an assistant coach when David played Little League baseball and Pee Wee football.

David's parents always thought baseball was the game he played best. When he came up to bat in Little League, they would cheer for David to hit a home run, and he often did — sometimes right handed and sometimes left handed.

David also liked to run races. When he competed, he

usually won. Afterwards, he loved to run into the house, pretend to sound a trumpet, and show his mom the newest first-place blue ribbon he had won.

When David was ten years old, he won the Virginia long-jump competition. That was a first-place blue ribbon that he was very proud of. David got to go to Kentucky with his coach to compete in the national competition. But as he was jumping in the finals, he fell. Surprisingly, he still placed second—in the nation!

When David saw his mother, though, he was reluctant to show her his ribbon. "I only won the red," he told her. But Mrs. Robinson told her son just how proud she was of him—not only because he had placed second but also because he had set such high standards for himself.

Unfortunately, not everything David did made his parents proud.

Chapter 5

Tempted to Steal

One day when he was ten years old, David wandered into a convenience store near the school bus stop with four-year-old Chuck. As they stood in front of a shelf full of candy, David looked around. *Was anybody watching?* he wondered.

I could steal some of this candy, David thought. Then he scooped up a handful of peanut butter cups and slipped them into his pocket. Glancing around, he was sure that no one saw him do it. David breathed a sigh of relief. *That was easy!* he thought, and he filled the other pocket.

David picked up a large candy bar and headed for the cash register. He tried to be casual as he placed the candy bar on the counter and handed the cashier the money.

"Son, will you step around here please!" The man's stern voice startled David. *How could he know?* David wondered. He had no idea that his bulging pocket had given him away.

Walking around the counter and facing that man was one of the worst moments of David's life. His parents had taught him how important it is to be honest. David knew he had done something really bad—and he had been caught.

The cashier called David's mother. "You'll have to come down to the store," she told Mrs. Robinson.

While the boys waited, Chuck kept telling David, "I'm going to tell! You are going to be in so much trouble."

By the time his mother arrived, David was crying. Other shoppers, some of them friends and neighbors, watched as David confessed and apologized. Then his mom took David home and spanked him. She even spanked Chuck for going along with the crime.

David's father was at sea, so David had to wait several weeks for him to get home. All that time, he worried. *What will my father do?*

But when his dad got home, he just talked to David. He didn't spank him. Mrs. Robinson had already done that. He also knew David felt really bad about what he had done. Just the waiting and worrying about what would happen when his father came home had been punishment enough for David.

Perhaps one reason David had been so worried about his punishment was because he'd never forgotten an earlier incident. When David was six or seven years old, he was watching television and absentmindedly began to poke a small pocketknife into the arm of his father's leather recliner. He wasn't trying to damage the chair on purpose. He just wasn't thinking about what he was doing.

When David got up from the chair, he looked down and saw what he had done. *Uh-oh,* he thought. *I did that!*

When David's father saw the ugly holes in his favorite chair, he was angry. "For every hole in this chair, I am going to spank you once," he said.

Poor David! That was a long spanking, but he learned an important lesson about how to treat other people's property.

David loved doing things with his father. In fact, whenever Ambrose Robinson worked around the house, David was usually by his side.

David watched as his father repaired their family cars. First, his dad would get a Chilton manual and read the instructions. Then he and David would put on some work gloves and crawl under the car. He taught David—and himself—to do most repairs.

When he needed a Phillips-head screwdriver, David's dad would send him for one. If he came back with the wrong one, his father would explain the difference and send David back for the right one.

In addition to repairing cars together, his dad bought electronic kits, and he and David put together radios and televisions by following the instructions that came with the kits.

David quickly learned to read instructions and follow them. He knew the difference between a transistor, a diode, and a capacitor. And he could identify all the tools in his dad's toolbox.

One day as he watched his father repair the family car, David wondered how he had learned to do so many things. "Dad, did you go to Dad School or something?" he asked.

When David, Kim, and Chuck got home from school each day, they would find their mother's chore list on either the refrigerator or the bulletin board. Sometimes David would cook dinner and Kim would wash the dishes. Or their mother might have instructed them to mow the lawn, trim the shrubs, vacuum the floors, or take out the garbage. Even when they were small, David's parents expected them to help out around the house.

David and his brother and sister were also expected to attend church and Bible study. When he was a baby, David's mom would leave him in the church nursery. But when he was three years old, he began staying with her during the services at least some of the time. If he misbehaved in church, she corrected him. She thought, *If he can't sit through a service for an hour or two, how will he sit still in kindergarten?*

Unless she had to work, Mrs. Robinson attended church every Sunday, and she always took her children with her. When they were teenagers, David, Kim, and Chuck started asking their mother, "Do we have to go?"

"Yes," Mrs. Robinson replied. "The Lord has been good to you this week. You owe it to him. We all need the Lord. And you might learn something new."

David's mother didn't make her children go to church

when they were sick. So sometimes they would tell her that they had a headache or a stomachache. She would answer, "Okay, but sick people don't get to have any activities. If we go skating or bowling or out for ice cream later today, you won't be able to go with us." Usually the "sick" child quickly recovered and went on to church.

One November day when David was in grade school, he came home and told his mother, "The teacher wants us to bring in four cans of food for the Thanksgiving baskets. And she wants us to give her the names of poor families. They'll select five names for the Thanksgiving baskets."

That afternoon, David's mom was tired. She worked every day, yet she was the mother who ended up driving David and a lot of other children to all the baseball and football practices. And it seemed like David, Kim, and Chuck were always bringing home notes from school asking for something.

Irritated, Mrs. Robinson told David, "Every time I turn around, it's give, give, give. This is the poor house right here. Our name needs to be in that drawing."

His mother didn't mean what she said, but David took her seriously. He put their name in the drawing at school for the Thanksgiving food baskets and in a similar basket at church.

David's mother was shocked when she received a phone call from the teacher. "Freda, you are trying to be slick. Why did you have David put your name in for a poor basket?"

That call was followed by another one from David's

Sunday school teacher. "Freda, we caught you! David put your name in for a Thanksgiving basket. But it didn't work!"

After Mrs. Robinson assured both the callers that the family was fine, and David had simply misunderstood, she had a talk with her son. "Mama, I was only trying to help. You told me this was the poor house," he told her.

Chapter 6

Quitting the Team

When David was eleven years old, his dad gave him his first golf lesson. They found themselves on a driving range with adult-sized clubs. To make matters worse, the clubs were made for a right-handed golfer, and David was left handed. Even with these challenges, David was a quick learner. Then with his dad telling him which club to use, David soon won a tournament for his age group.

David also continued to do well in school. As part of his sixth- and seventh-grade gifted program, he took courses in speed-reading, algebra, and advanced math at a local junior college. He was so good in math that by the time he was in junior high, his teacher was allowing him to grade papers. The teacher would drive by the Robinson house and drop off all the papers for David to work on.

One day the teacher forgot to include the answer sheet. David called and told him that it was missing. "You don't need the master sheet. You already know all the answers," his teacher told him. And he was right. David answered all the questions and graded the papers correctly.

In the eighth grade, David had a teacher he really didn't like. So on his first report card, he earned one A, two Bs, and one C. His parents grounded him for six weeks. Until he brought home an acceptable grade report, David could not leave his house or yard after school.

David was expected to do his best, and a C was obviously not the best that David Robinson—or any Robinson—could do. David did not know any other family who took such drastic action over one low grade. But David learned that his parents would not accept less than his best.

If you had seen David Robinson's first attempt to play on an organized basketball team, you would never have guessed that he would one day be a basketball star. In junior high, David made the team but spent most of his time on the bench.

David was five-feet, nine-inches tall—pretty good for a junior high student. And he was a good athlete. But he hadn't played much basketball at home or in the neighborhood, so he wasn't always sure what he should be doing on the court.

He went to basketball practice every day and attended all the games. But David hadn't learned the flashy playground moves so many of the other kids had mastered, so he was reluctant to handle the ball. While his teammates loved to dribble and drive and shoot, David preferred to play defense and not be the center of attention.

In the locker room, David also felt out of place. The other players were "cool" kids, and David was a bookworm—a "brain." At practices and in the locker room, the other guys talked about girls. David was much more interested in books. He didn't start dating girls until after he graduated from high school.

Finally, David grew tired of feeling awkward around the other players on his team. He was frustrated that he spent so much time practicing and so little time playing in games. So he went to his father. "Dad," he said, "I want to quit the basketball team. I'm not getting any playing time. They only put me in when we're twenty points up, and there are two minutes left."

David and his father spent only a couple of minutes talking about it. Mr. Robinson felt that if David wanted to spend his time studying rather than playing basketball, he was not going to argue with him. "That's fine, David," his dad said. "You don't have to play."

Then David had to talk to his mother about it.

"Mom, I don't want to be a bench warmer," he told her. "It's a waste of my time."

His mother listened to David's reasons. What he had to say satisfied her.

"To be a quitter is to be a loser," David's mom responded. "But sometimes you need to quit some things. You have to be level headed about it. There's a thin line between quitting and being a quitter. If you can recognize the line that says, 'Quit now while you're ahead,' you'll be okay."

That was the first time David ever quit any team or activity. That basketball team went on to win the city championship, but David was never sorry he made that decision.

When David was fifteen years old, his dad bought a large-screen television kit. This was different from any of the other kits that he and David had put together. For one thing, this one cost a lot more. And father and son had never tackled anything quite so complicated.

The Heathkit was delivered to the house while David's dad was still at sea. He had planned for them to work on it as soon as he got home. But a couple of weeks before his dad was due back, David opened the big box that had been sitting in the family den. He started putting one of the smaller boards together.

When his mother got home from work that day, Kim met her as she got out of her car. "Mom, I tried to stop him! David is in a world of trouble."

Mrs. Robinson was startled. "What happened?" she wanted to know.

"David got into that box, and he is messing with Daddy's television," Kim explained.

"David and his daddy will build that when his daddy gets back," her mother replied.

"Mom, you don't understand. He's got a whole board done."

Mrs. Robinson headed into the house to investigate

and found David in the den. Kim was right. David had opened the box and was working on it.

"David, do you know how much that kit cost?" his mother wanted to know.

"Mom, I know what I'm doing," David insisted. He kept on working.

"You had better not solder on that board unless you are absolutely sure. It will be ruined if you are wrong," his mother warned him. David was using a soldering gun, a tool that melts metal pieces together. If he soldered the wrong parts together, the television would never work.

"Mom, you worry too much," David answered. He kept on reading the instructions and working, just like he had seen his father do with smaller kits.

When Freda went to pick up her husband at his ship, she was nervous. "Honey, don't get mad, but David put your kit together."

"Oh, I wouldn't worry about it. He knows what he's doing." David's dad was a lot calmer than his mother. And he was right!

At home, David's dad had a chance to look the television over. It wasn't working, but David insisted that the kit was missing a piece. His father checked and decided that David's conclusion was correct.

Mr. Robinson went to the Heathkit store and picked up the missing piece. As soon as that part was in place, the new television worked. It had a really good picture for a six-foot screen. And the Robinsons used that television for many years.

Some time later, David and his dad went back to the Heathkit store to make some purchases. David noticed a frustrated technician working on a demonstration model, walked over to watch, and began to advise him. When the man took David's advice, the problem was solved.

Chapter 7

Decision Time

Ambrose Robinson was not about to buy his daughter, Kimberly, a moped even though he knew how badly she wanted one. But Kim wouldn't let him forget about it. She kept talking and begging. She explained, in detail, how useful the bike would be. But her dad thought it would be too dangerous, and he was sure she was too young.

Finally, Freda came up with a plan. They would tell Kim that she could have a moped, but she would have to pay for it herself. The moped cost $600, and Kim made only one dollar an hour babysitting. It would take her a long time to earn that much money. Maybe by then, her mother thought, she would lose interest. But her parents agreed that if she could save that much money, she would be allowed to buy a moped. They presented their plan to Kim, and she agreed. Then she went to work!

Six hundred dollars was a lot of babysitting. But Kim made it. She worked and saved, and finally, she bought the moped. She was so proud!

Kim rode that moped all around the neighborhood, and she took good care of it. She kept it clean and polished and parked in the garage out of the weather. Every now and then, she even let David take it for a ride. He loved it!

Kim kept the moped until she got her driver's license and was able to drive the car. Then she decided to give the moped to David for his birthday.

David was thrilled. What a birthday present! He rode the moped up and down the street, telling everyone he saw that the moped now belonged to him. He was convinced Kimberly was the best sister in the world.

One afternoon several months later, Mrs. Robinson came home to find her daughter in tears.

"Mama," Kimberly cried, "David sold the moped for $90!"

Kimberly was hurt and angry. How had David dared to sell the moped that meant so much to her? And for next to nothing!

"I wouldn't have given it to him if I'd known he didn't want it," she told her mother.

Freda went to talk to David about it. David told her that since the moped was his, he thought he could do anything he wanted with it.

His mother thought about it. She knew the boy to whom David had sold the moped, and she knew his mother. If she talked to them, she knew that she could make arrangements for David to buy the moped back. The boy who bought it knew that the moped was worth a lot more than he had paid for it. It would only be fair for Mrs. Robinson to get the moped back for David. But what would he learn about what he had done?

David's mother made up her mind and said to him, "I am not going to ask that boy to give the moped back. I'm going to let him keep it. But your bike is broken, and your dad and I will not fix it. We won't take you anywhere either, so don't even ask us to drive you. From now on, you will have to walk wherever you go. And when your $90 runs out, you're on your own."

David was quickly sorry that he had sold the moped. He got very tired of walking. And his sister Kimberly would have nothing to do with him for weeks.

While David was in high school, his father retired from the Navy and took a job consulting on government contracts. Mr. Robinson's new career took him to Crystal City, Virginia, near Washington, D.C., about 185 miles from their home in Virginia Beach. At first, he commuted to Crystal City. He would stay in an apartment near his work during the week and come home on the weekends. Finally, after a year the Robinsons bought a house in Woodbridge, Virginia, near his job, and on October 31, 1982, the family moved to their new home.

David struggled with the decision to move. He was a senior in high school. His school was reputed to be in one of the nation's best school districts. And he had good friends in Virginia Beach. He knew what his class schedule would be. He had been looking forward to taking calculus and was signed up for several advanced classes. David told his parents he didn't want to move. Since it seemed to make sense for him to stay behind and finish high school, they made arrangements for David to live with a family friend.

David's mother cried the night they left him behind. As soon as they were gone, David knew he had made a mistake. He missed his family and wanted to live with them. But he didn't know how to tell his parents that he had changed his mind.

Each morning before school, David would call and talk to his mother. She could tell he was feeling home-sick. So after two weeks, she asked David if he wanted to join the family in Woodbridge. The words were barely out of her mouth when David answered, "Yes, Ma'am!"

Freda immediately called her husband with the news.

"Why are you calling me?" Ambrose told her. "Just go get him."

David's mom called her lonely son. "Tell the guidance counselor I said to get all your papers together because you're moving. I'll be down there in three hours."

"Oh, yes, ma'am!" David answered. Before his mom arrived, David had his bags packed and his paperwork done.

"Mama," he told her, "I'm so glad you came. I missed you."

The next day, David's dad took him to register at his new school. They went first to Garfield High only a few blocks from their new home. But they learned that their neighborhood had been re-zoned, and David had to go to Osbourne Park High School in Manassas, thirteen miles away.

This did not seem like good news, but they drove to Osbourne Park. That's where David met Art Payne, who became his guidance counselor and his basketball coach. Payne took one look at the six-foot, seven-inch new kid and asked David, "Why don't you try out for the basketball team?"

The rest of that day, the students kept telling David, "You've got to play basketball!" Everyone was friendly, and David didn't want to say no.

That afternoon, he watched the team practice. He even made a few shots in his stocking feet. The next day he took his physical examination and started to practice with the team. The team had been practicing together for a while, but had not yet played a game.

They had another six-foot, seven-inch player who played center. But that player had been injured, and David suddenly became the team's starting center.

In the first game of the season, David scored 14 points and grabbed 14 rebounds. Coach Payne could see that David had lots of raw talent. He had never coached another big man who was such a natural at handling the ball. But it was obvious David had not played enough to develop his basketball instincts.

Coach Payne asked a former college basketball center to come to practices and work with David on fundamentals. Since David was a quick learner, he developed rapidly during the season. David averaged 14 points per game and made the All-Area and All-District teams.

But basketball was nothing more than a game to David. With college just around the corner, he had a future to plan. And he never expected basketball to be part of it.

Chapter 8

Basketball or Education?

Because he hadn't played basketball until his senior year of high school, David was surprised that so many college recruiters showed an interest in him. But the combination of his size and impressive high school academic record (plus a score of 1320 on the SAT) drew a lot of attention. Harvard, Holy Cross, and George Mason University all expressed interest.

But part way through David's senior basketball season, Paul Evans, the basketball coach at the United States Naval Academy in Annapolis, Maryland, received a phone call from a Navy officer who lived in David's hometown. "There's a big kid playing for Osbourne Park," he said. "You need to come down and see him."

So Coach Evans drove down to northern Virginia to take a look. "David was a skinny kid who could run," he remembered, "but he couldn't do much else." Coach Evans wasn't impressed.

However, Evans followed David's performance for the remainder of the season. He saw enough improvement to convince him that in time David might become a decent college athlete. And he could tell David was interested in the Academy.

"David wanted a good education," Evans said. "His father had a career in the Navy, so I think the idea of becoming a naval officer appealed to him. The education certainly did."

Coach Evans had David figured right—at least about one thing. David was actually more interested in the quality of the education he would receive than he was in the school's basketball program. All his life he had figured he would become an engineer or some kind of scientist. If being good enough to stick a ball through a hoop and tall enough to keep others from doing it got him a college scholarship—great! But David was much more concerned about getting an education that would prepare him for his future career.

Like Coach Evans, David's father had also watched the remarkable improvement in his son's basketball skills and began to think David had a real future in the game. But if that were true, it would be better for David to go somewhere besides the Naval Academy, because after graduation he would be required to spend five years in the Navy.

When Ambrose Robinson visited the Virginia Military Institute (VMI) with David, he was convinced it would be the perfect school for his son. VMI offered both military school discipline and an excellent engineering department. The small campus seemed like a great environment for learning. David's dad also liked the coaches. He was impressed with the fact that they ran a basketball program that would enable his son to go right into the pros after graduation.

David liked VMI well enough. But he was practically awestruck when he came home from a weekend visit to the Naval Academy. "Wow, Mom!" he exclaimed. "The lab set up is better than any college I've visited. They have so much equipment I couldn't believe it. But I just can't make up my mind."

"David," his mother said, "Annapolis sounds wonderful. I like the Naval Academy. But the question is, which school do you like best?"

"Dad likes VMI," he replied.

"David," his mother told him, "go where you want to go, not where I want you to go or where your daddy wants you to go. You have to decide which school you think would be best for you."

David thought he knew the answer already. "Probably the Naval Academy. Mom, you should see their labs!"

But David still hadn't given the schools or his parents his final answer. "I was still torn," he says. "I knew it needed to be my decision, but part of me wanted my parents to make it for me. Or at least tell me what they thought I should do. They kept saying they wanted me to decide, but I could tell they each had their own ideas."

David had always tried to be an obedient son who never wanted to disappoint his dad. So when his father pressed his son to tell him what he was thinking, David told him he thought VMI would be a great school. His father heard, or thought he heard, David saying, "I guess I'll go to VMI."

So Mr. Robinson phoned VMI, and three of their coaches drove down to sign the skinny, raw basketball recruit who'd only played one year of high school ball. The VMI recruiters were in the den talking to David and his dad when Mrs. Robinson came downstairs and walked into the room. "What's going on?" she asked.

"These are the people from VMI who have come to sign David," Mr. Robinson told her.

"No, they're not!" Mrs. Robinson said.

David's father and the VMI coaches were surprised. They thought the matter was settled. Everyone turned to look at David.

After a long and awkward silence, David told them, "I'm going to the Naval Academy." Then he thanked the men for coming.

After the disappointed VMI coaches had gone, Mrs. Robinson asked her son, "You're not going to Navy because I like it are you?"

"Mom," he told her, "it's the best place for me."

"You need to be sure you're going there for the right reasons," she said.

"I am," he replied.

Mrs. Robinson felt like dancing. But she didn't because she realized she needed to cheer up her husband.

"The education he will get at the Naval Academy will far outweigh the five years of quick money he might make playing basketball. Besides, basketball is secondary."

"You're right," Mr. Robinson agreed. He'd always believed that education was more important than sports. He had often told his children so. He was less disappointed than he was embarrassed about inviting the VMI recruiters to come before he really understood what David wanted to do. He always did believe the final decision was his son's to make. After all, David was the one who would have to live with the choice.

David wasn't so sure he'd made the right decision on the hot July day in 1983 when he reported to the Naval Academy in Annapolis. Starting the day dressed in jeans and a casual shirt, David spent most of the morning with his new classmates—filling out forms, receiving uniforms, and finally getting dormitory assignments. "I remember standing in all these different lines waiting to go to all these different places," he says. "It was one of the longest days of my life."

And it would get longer. At the end of the afternoon, the new midshipmen were finally sworn in. Then they were sworn at.

"Suddenly, all the upperclassmen started yelling at us and telling us where to go," David recalled. "Earlier in the day, they'd been polite. But once we were sworn in, they weren't polite at all. I remember all these people yelling at me and thinking, *What have I gotten myself into? Was it a mistake to come here?*" Sleep didn't come easily that first night.

Basketball or Education?

Navy Midshipman 1st Class David Robinson poses aboard a ship in Annapolis, MD.

The physical demands were also tough. To start with, all midshipmen were expected to swim one hundred meters—four lengths of the pool. David couldn't make it. So he was assigned to a swimming class where he had to swim for forty minutes at a time. He also had to dive off a tower thirty feet high. It would take him a while to conquer his fear and learn to make the dive without thinking.

For a long time David wondered about the wisdom of his decision. "That first month I was at school, I didn't know if I was going to cut it," he admits. If the physical stuff didn't kill him, the academic demands threatened to do him in. "Going in, I felt pretty good about my qualifications," he said. "But almost immediately it hit me. Wow! There are a lot of really smart people here. It seemed like everyone I talked to was first or second in his high school class and had scored 1500 or more on their SAT.

"Suddenly, I felt like I was down at the bottom of the barrel. I knew I was going to have to work harder than I had in high school just to keep up."

Would he be able to do it? David had felt convinced that Navy was the place for him, but now he began to question his college decision. *Maybe I made a big mistake*, he thought. And he seriously began to think about quitting.

Chapter 9

Naval Academy Discipline

David honestly didn't know if he could handle the hazing and the demanding physical conditioning the freshmen "plebes" had to endure to prove they were tough enough to become Navy officers.

The daily schedule was bad enough. David and the other midshipmen had to get up, shower, shave, dress, eat breakfast, and report for daily marching drills by 7:30 a.m. Then they attended four hours of classes, ate lunch, and went back to classes until late afternoon. In the evening they ate dinner, endured marching drills, and then spent time studying before bedtime.

The classes themselves were tough—thermodynamics, navigation, advanced calculus, physics, computer science, electrical engineering, weapons, history of science and technology, contemporary American literature, advanced computer programming, celestial navigation, advanced numerical analysis, computer data structures, partial differential equations, and economic geography. The homework load nearly overwhelmed him that first term. "Most days we had too much," David says. "The rest of the time we had way too much."

"In high school I had taken things for granted," he says. "My classes had always been easy. I didn't have to study for them. Then I got to the Naval Academy, and I didn't have time to do anything else. Wow! There was so much work to do. I had to focus. But I soon realized how much stronger that was making me as a student and as a person."

The lessons his parents had taught came back to him. And he decided to stick it out.

David shared a room with Carl "Hootie" Liebert in Bancroft Hall where 137 other midshipmen also lived. The dorm had no TVs and only one phone. Plebes were never allowed to leave campus to shop, see a movie, or even grab a McDonald's hamburger except on special occasions. Even then they had to ask for and receive official permission. So there weren't a lot of options on campus to distract the students from their studies.

But David needed all of the focus and discipline he could get. Once the basketball team began working out, he would face all the academic challenges the other students did *plus* he had to fit daily practice into an already packed schedule. Then he would have to find ways to keep up his class work while playing a 30-game basketball season with evening and weekend road trips all over the country.

David planned to play basketball, but he wasn't at all sure how seriously he would take the game. After all, he'd only played one year in high school. "I figured basketball would just be an outlet for me—a change of pace from studies," David says.

But basketball at the college level proved to be a tougher challenge and a bigger distraction than David had anticipated. From his first practice scrimmages, Coach Evans had David line up against the team's best player, six-foot, seven-inch Vernon Butler, who was nicknamed Captain Crunch for his physical style of play. He and David also battled each other in rebounding drills.

"I got beat up every day in practice," David recalls. "I caught a lot of elbows and spent a lot of time protecting my nose. The game just didn't come naturally to me, so basketball seemed like more work than fun."

Keeping up with academics was also more difficult than he'd expected. "You get out of practice and you're tired," he says. "You wake up in the morning and you're already tired from what you did the day before."

Paul Evans demanded and expected total dedication from his players. But David just didn't share his enthusiasm for the game. Pete Herrmann, the assistant coach during David's first three years, says it was obvious that basketball wasn't that important to David. "There wasn't much he liked about his freshman year, including practice. Later he told me he would sit in his math class sixth period and say to himself, 'Oh, brother, I have to go to basketball practice today.'"

David got so tired playing basketball and trying to

keep up with his studies that he kept falling asleep in class. He even slept standing up. It got so bad that Naval Academy officials thought he might have a medical problem. When David broke his hand boxing in a physical education class, they realized what was happening. The x-rays of David's broken hand showed a significant gap in his bones—David was still growing. In fact, he was growing so fast, his body needed extra rest to keep up.

So the broken bone was not bad news at all for the Navy basketball coaches and doctors. In fact, the doctor who called David's parents about his injury was excited about what they'd discovered.

"David will probably be a seven footer," he told them. If that were true, it would indeed be amazing news for the team.

Because of the close quarters aboard ships and submarines, the Navy wanted most of its officers to be less than six-feet, six-inches tall. A small percentage of each Academy class could be as tall as six feet, eight inches but no taller. At six feet, seven-and-a-half inches, David had been just under the upper limit when he took his entrance physical in February of his senior year of high school. But once accepted, midshipmen can't become ineligible if they grow. And grow David did. He was six feet, nine inches by the time he enrolled, and now the x-rays indicated that he would soon be more than seven feet tall.

The coaches had hoped David would become a decent, small forward. They were absolutely thrilled at the prospect of him growing into the big-time center Navy had never had.

Manny Millan/Getty Images

In the 1986 NCAA Eastern Regional playoffs against Duke, David prevents an opponent from dunking.

However, they soon began to wonder if those dreams would ever come true. David had an unimpressive freshman season. He missed the first four games because of his broken hand. When he did come back, he wasn't a starter and didn't play much. He averaged 7.6 points after playing about 13 minutes a game.

Yet Coach Evans remained convinced of David's potential. He liked the way such a big kid could get up and down the court. But he didn't like the fact that David seemed lazy in practice. He couldn't figure out how to motivate him.

Some of the other players on the team must have seen David's potential as well. They kidded him and called him "Country" when they learned he'd never flown in an airplane or been inside a hotel or a bar.

But they quickly noticed how graceful and athletic he was. His roommate Hootie Leibert recalls a required three-week course in gymnastics. "Dave was so big I didn't think he could do it. But after the rest of us looked bad, he got up on the parallel bars and started making these fancy moves and doing all sorts of stuff. It only took him a week to do everything required to get an A in the course.

"He was so good at everything, it was disgusting," Hootie says. "I wished there was just one sport I could beat him in. He could shoot a great round of golf, and he played tennis well. I thought maybe I could take him at squash since the court is so little. But he beat me at that, too."

As the season progressed, David's basketball skills

steadily improved. He played well enough to be named rookie of the year in the conference. Navy's basketball team won twenty games for the first time in the school's history. By the end of the year, David had grown to six-feet, ten-inches tall.

The coaches were more convinced than ever that David had the potential to be something special on the basketball court. But head coach Paul Evans grew even more frustrated that David didn't seem to understand or appreciate his great physical talent. The coaches hadn't yet found a good strategy for motivating him.

Evans had tried to push David in practice, working him hard and yelling at him whenever he thought his big man was slacking off. While he had seen steady improvement during the season, sometimes the coach felt his freshman center just tuned him out.

Not knowing what else to do, Evans finally went to David's father. "How can I motivate your son?" he asked. Mr. Robinson wasn't sure either.

Finally the coach called David into his office. He told the young player he might someday make a lot of money as a professional basketball player if he would work harder to develop his game.

David wasn't convinced. He still wasn't sure he even wanted to play basketball.

Chapter 10

Tallest Player in Navy History

David did, however, begin working with Navy's strength coach, lifting weights and running to stay in shape during the off season. He also spent the summer playing against outstanding college and pro stars in the Washington Urban Coalition League.

By the time he returned to Annapolis the fall of his sophomore year, David had developed an outstanding shooting touch. He seemed quicker and more agile despite the fact that he had added 25 or 30 pounds of muscle and had grown to six-feet, eleven-inches tall.

The coaches were more excited than ever about David's physical development. He was now the tallest player in Navy history. If they could find a way to get him to make the most of his skills, they believed their team could actually improve on last year's 24–8 record.

That David hadn't played much in high school was

turning out to be an advantage. Coach Evans liked the fact that his young center was still learning the game. "It was like coaching a ninth or tenth grader," he says. Because David hadn't already played for five or six years, he didn't have bad habits on the floor that he needed to break. "Plus it's a lot easier to teach a kid with great intelligence, which David had."

Still, David's performance was not impressive during the first couple of games that season. Then in game three against American University, he broke out for 29 points and 11 rebounds, leading the way for an impressive 84–68 Navy win. After that game, American's coach said about David, "He's one of the top big men in the east."

A few days later, David really caught fire at a tournament in Illinois. Against Southern Illinois University (SIU), he scored 31 points and snatched 13 rebounds from SIU's six-foot, eleven-inch center. And the next night against Western Illinois, David did even better with 37 points and 17 rebounds.

David couldn't believe what he'd done. "It was the first time I got an idea of what I could do," he says.

Hootie Liebert remembers that after the Western Illinois game, David turned to him and said, "Wow! I can play!"

In four games that week, including the two games of the tournament, David scored a total of 115 points, grabbed 52 rebounds, and won the Saluki Shootout MVP award. David wasn't the only one impressed with his performances. Navy's opponents just couldn't stop him. He was too quick for their big men to cover and too tall for the little guys. He outran the guards down the floor on fast breaks and then out jumped the front court guys for rebounds and dunks.

The media noticed, too. Newspapers and magazines all over the country ran stories about Navy's amazing center. *Sports Illustrated* named him "Player of the Week." To David's surprise, it seemed he'd suddenly become a big-time player.

"I'd never thought of myself that way," he admits. "In high school, basketball was just something I experimented with." Now, at last, David realized he had the potential to be good—if he worked at it. Yet he still frustrated his coaches when he told the media, "If I don't become a big star, it isn't that big a deal. I still play to have fun."

After the Illinois tournament, the Navy team went almost four weeks without any games, to give players the chance to study and take final exams. David tried to focus on schoolwork, but it was during this time that sportswriters from various papers began to speculate that he might consider leaving Navy at the end of the school year.

The experts were saying he was good enough to play professional ball. And if he transferred to another school, he wouldn't have to do his five years of military service. He could go to the NBA as soon as he graduated.

So, naturally, reporters began asking David about his plans. "When people bring up pro basketball to me, I laugh," he told them. "I don't think of myself that way.

Richard Drew/AP Photo

A proud David holds his Eastman Award that he received in 1987 for being the college basketball player of the year.

Basketball is just one of the things I do." People were talking about him transferring, but he wasn't considering it. In fact, he said if people hadn't started asking him about it, "I never would have thought about it at all."

But the flood of speculation forced David to think

about it. Almost every day someone reminded him by writing about how much money he could make as a professional basketball player. The idea of making a good living playing a game was tempting. He admitted that when people talked about playing basketball for hundreds of thousands of dollars a year, "You can't help but have it on your mind."

David also told interviewers, "Maybe I don't think I'm as good as other people seem to think I am. Right now I don't see any reason to leave Navy. It's a tough place, but I'm happy here."

When the season resumed in January, David led Navy to ten straight victories. The midshipmen began attracting their biggest crowds ever. It seemed everyone turned out to watch David Robinson play. They were seldom disappointed.

Navy finished the season with an impressive 22–5 record. Then they won three post-season games in a row to take the East Coast Athletic Conference (ECAC) South—the first Navy team since 1960 to be invited to play in the NCAA tournament. They defeated a favored Louisiana State University team in the opening round before finally being eliminated by Maryland. It was an incredible accomplishment for the team and an impressive achievement for David.

Finishing the season with 756 points, David broke a school record that had stood for thirty-one years. David also set Navy records for field goals, 30-point games, and rebounding. He received all-conference honors and was voted ECAC South Player of the Year.

By the time the season ended, David was seven-feet, one-inch tall. There was no longer any question that he was a legitimate pro prospect. And he was forced to make a decision about his future.

If he came back to Annapolis the next fall for his junior year, he would be expected to graduate and was then required to serve out his five years in the Navy. Did he want to risk delaying or losing a possible NBA career? Or should he transfer to a big basketball school, lose one year of college eligibility, but work on his game and try to improve his potential and future earnings?

David knew this was a big decision. Notre Dame, UCLA, Kentucky, Georgetown, and Indiana were glad to take him.

He discussed the pros and cons with his parents a number of times over the next few months. They talked to the Naval Academy superintendent who suggested that David might not be required to serve all five years. He hinted that because David was so tall, he might not have to serve at all, or his term of service might be limited to two years. But he couldn't offer any guarantees.

There were no guarantees if David transferred either. Yes, it could mean millions of dollars in just two or three years. But NCAA rules would require him to sit out a season, and who knew how much or how well he might play once he became eligible?

David told Coach Evans, "I like basketball, and it's a challenge. But it is just one part of my life. If I have to, I can live without it."

David remembers what he was thinking at the time.

"My first two years at the Naval Academy had been a great experience. The education was obviously top notch. And I enjoyed the people, going out on the ships during the summer, and getting that experience. The demands were making me a better, more disciplined person. And I needed that."

He was a little afraid that if he transferred to another school where no one required or expected him to go to class every day, he might be tempted to blow off his academics. "I knew the standard the Navy held me to was something I really needed and now appreciated. When I was on the campus at Annapolis, I felt almost isolated from the world. I could concentrate and learn there. There was no partying. No fraternities or sororities. No social causes to get involved in. No distractions. Just time to study and get your work done."

It was a tough choice — one that kept him lying awake at night staring at the ceiling of his dorm room. If he stayed at the Academy and graduated, he'd be guaranteed a job in the Navy that paid $20,000 a year plus food, housing, and travel. He'd probably be twenty-seven years old before he got a chance to play in the NBA; his skills might be too rusty by then.

David says, "I knew the decision could mean a lot of money. And people think you will automatically be happy if you have a lot of money. But I didn't necessarily believe that was true."

When David finally made his decision, he asked a Navy spokesman to read this statement to reporters: "The Academy has been good for me, and I want the chance to receive a degree from here. Pro ball? I guess I still have a hard time visualizing myself playing at that level with all those great players. I want to improve on what we accomplished this year. Everyone is saying I'm great, but who can you listen to? I'm in control. I'm doing what I want to do. I have no regrets. I came here for academics, but all my goals got cloudy. The press confused me a lot. Basketball came so fast. It really just came together this year. I'm still in my early stages. I don't know how much basketball means to me right now."

That was it. David had made his decision. He had chosen academics over sports.

David never anticipated the reaction. He was praised in speeches and editorials all over America for his character. People were more impressed than ever. Here was a young man who chose commitment, loyalty, learning, and national service over celebrity and wealth.

Ironically, that decision made him more famous than ever. He tried to downplay what he'd done by saying he'd merely listened to his heart. His experience with the Navy had been good so far, "so I went with the flow. Fulfilling my commitment simply felt like the right thing to do."

Indeed, it eventually turned out to be the right thing for David Robinson to do—in more ways than one. But sometimes over the next few years he couldn't help but wonder if he'd made a mistake.

Chapter 11

"The Admiral"

David felt like he was playing basketball in an oven. The sweat dripped off his nose, his chin, and his elbows. He could feel it rolling down his arms, his legs, and his back. It was 105 degrees, and his United States' teammates never seemed to let up in their preparations for an international tournament event called the Jones Cup. David was impressed by the level of commitment he was witnessing. Here were some of the best college players in the country, "and these guys were busting it every day," David says. "They never wanted to stop playing. It was kind of inspiring." He was getting a glimpse of what it took to be one of the best, and the experience gave him increased confidence.

Back at the Naval Academy the following fall, David's teammates noticed a change in his attitude. His friend and roommate Hootie Liebert told reporters, "David's talking about how he can't wait to practice. I've never heard him say that before."

Experts ranked Navy among the top 20 teams in the country in a pre-season poll. Many people were calling David the nation's best college center. Coach Evans continued to believe he could be—but only if he started working harder. David still had a tendency to let up and coast unless his competition really pushed him.

When his coach tried to push him, David resented it. Evans was an old-fashioned screamer. He seldom had an encouraging word. The Navy coach could swear like a sailor.

One day when Coach Evans thought David was slacking off in practice, he blew up, pointed at the door, and told him, "Get out of the gym!" He kicked his star out of practice.

David left. But he was more mad than motivated. He figured, *The coach is playing mind games with me. It may work with other guys, but it's not going to work with me.*

David's father knew his son didn't appreciate being yelled at, but he felt on occasion it may have helped. "There were probably times," Mr. Robinson says, "when David buckled down and tried harder in order to prove something to his coach. He would think, *I'll show him!* and then he did."

As a junior in the 1985–86 season, David averaged 22.7 points a game and led the nation with 13.0 rebounds and 5.9 blocks a game. He set NCAA records for blocked shots in a game, season, and career. He was named to numerous All-America teams and made Player of the Year in his conference again. He became such a commanding presence on Navy's basketball court that he was nicknamed "The Admiral" and "The Aircraft Carrier."

Navy made the NCAA tournament for the second year in a row. They won handily in the first round, then faced a talented Syracuse team who boasted two future first-round NBA draft picks—Rony Seikaly and Dwayne "Pearl" Washington. David scored 35 points, hauled down 11 rebounds, blocked 7 shots, and held Seikaly to just 4 points in what was a huge upset win for Navy.

In their next game, David scored the winning basket with six seconds left in the game. Navy defeated Cleveland State 71–70. One more win, and the surprising Middies would be going to the Final Four. But Duke squelched that dream and ended Navy's incredible tournament run by easily winning the next game. For David it was such a disappointing end to a promising season that he complained. He accused the team of playing like a bunch of wimps and refused to talk to the press for several weeks.

Neither David's teammates nor his coach took offense at his criticism. They saw it as a sign that David was caring more about basketball than he ever had before.

The summer before his senior year, David played on the U.S. National Basketball team in the World Championships held in Madrid, Spain. Once again he rose to the challenge of playing alongside and against some of the best competitors in the world as he led the U.S. to a win over the Soviets in the first American World

"The Admiral"

As a center for the U.S. Naval Academy, David goes up for a shot in Alumni Hall in Annapolis, MD.

Championship performance since 1954. David also spent two weeks in Hawaii that summer on naval duty, serving aboard an American aircraft carrier.

When he returned from all his travels to Annapolis that fall, David received encouraging news. Napoleon McCallum, Navy's star running back, had been selected by the Los Angeles Raiders in the National Football League's draft the previous spring. When Napoleon was stationed in Long Beach, California, not far from the Raiders' training camp, the Navy had given him permission to play football with the Raiders on Sundays. If McCallum could play football, that meant perhaps David would be given the chance to play part time for an NBA team while he was completing his required military service.

David already knew he would be stationed at some naval base after he graduated because he was too tall to serve aboard a ship. A week's assignment the previous summer aboard a submarine with six-foot ceilings and tiny living quarters convinced David and his superiors that he couldn't be expected to live constantly hunched over. One training flight folded into the cockpit of a Navy fighter plane proved he couldn't fly either. Shore duty it would have to be.

Meanwhile, he had one more season of college basketball to look forward to. Coach Evans had taken a job at the University of Pittsburgh, so his assistant Pete Herrmann took over at Navy. David thought this was a good change. There were occasions during his senior season when David realized he might have pushed a little harder with Evans yelling at him, and may have even missed the tongue-lashings. But for the most part, David related better to Herrmann's quieter and more positive style as he slowly learned how to motivate himself. David usually wanted to work in order to please his new coach. He was now enjoying basketball so much and playing so well that the idea of joining the NBA seemed more appealing than ever. He found it tougher and tougher to not know if the Navy would require him to serve five years or two years after graduation.

"Last year I was up in the air about the pros," he admitted to the press. "But, yes, I want to play now. God gave me the height and ability to play, and I want to—very much. If I had known two years ago that I would feel this way now, I might have made a different decision and not stayed here."

David began the season with a bang, pouring in 36 points in an opening loss to North Carolina State and then leading Navy to a one-point overtime win over Michigan State in which he scored a new career high of 43 points. But as the season progressed, David found it difficult to concentrate on basketball or his classes. He had learned that the Navy was in the process of making a final decision regarding his length of service. The question had stirred up a lot of debate around the country. So he worried that the Navy might make an example of him and insist on a five-year commitment.

But on January 9, 1987, Navy Secretary John Lehman announced that David would have to serve two years after graduation. During that time, he would be allowed to play in the 1987 Pan American Games and the 1988 Summer Olympics. After he completed his two years of active duty, he would have to serve four years in the Naval Reserve, which would involve three weeks of training each summer.

Relieved, David went out and celebrated the Navy's decision by scoring 45 points and grabbing 21 rebounds in his team's next game against James Madison. He went on to complete another impressive season, leading the nation again in blocked shots while ranking third in scoring and fourth in rebounding. He became the first college player ever to combine 2,500 career points, 1,300 rebounds, and 60 percent shooting from the floor. He was named to every All-America team after setting 33 Navy records and launching the Middies into another NCAA playoff appearance.

Unfortunately, Navy drew the highly ranked University of Michigan Wolverines in the opening round of the NCAA East Regional in Charlotte, North Carolina. The fans stood and clapped when it was announced that David had won the Naismith Award as College Player of the Year. And then he really gave them something to cheer about.

Number 50 dazzled everyone in the building by scoring 50 points that night—a career high. The fact that the rest of Navy's team was no match for the supertalented Michigan squad took nothing away from David's performance.

The score wasn't close when Coach Herrmann took his star center out of the game with two seconds

Jerry Wachter/Getty Images

In David's final college game against the University of Michigan, he scored 50 points, a career high. He received a standing ovation from the audience, and a player from Michigan ran over and shook his hand.

left—just in case anyone wanted to applaud his effort. Everyone did. The fans' standing ovation went on for several minutes as one by one the Michigan players ran over to shake his hand and his Navy teammates jumped off their chairs to bear hug him.

David Robinson's spectacular college career was over.

Chapter 12

Drafted by the Spurs

After Navy was eliminated from the NCAA tournament, David returned to Annapolis and worked hard to catch up on his schoolwork. His grade point average had dropped during his senior year. "My mother is all over me because of that," he said.

There was good news and bad news that spring about his professional basketball prospects. The experts said he was certain to be the first player chosen in the 1987 NBA draft in June. They agreed he was by far the most talented player available. And even if he could only play part time for the first couple of years, most teams still wanted him.

That was the good news.

The bad news was that the new Secretary of the Navy felt being an officer was a 24-hour-a-day job. He did not want Navy athletes to play professional sports until they completed their military service. That meant David wouldn't be able to join the NBA, even part time, until his two-year commitment was over.

But even that bad news turned out to be good for David. Since he couldn't play for two years anyway, he wouldn't have to play for the first team to draft him. If for some reason he didn't like the team or wasn't willing to accept their contract, he could turn down their offer and go into the draft again the following year. If he didn't sign with the second team to draft him, he would only have to wait until his two-year service commitment was up, and he would be a free agent, able to sign with any team he wanted. He could choose to wait for a bidding war to see which team would pay him the most money. The Navy might not let him play pro ball for two years, but when it came to the future, he was suddenly very much in the driver's seat. In two years he could be playing with Michael Jordan's Bulls, Magic Johnson's Lakers, Larry Bird's Celtics, or any other player or team he might choose.

When the NBA held their annual draft lottery on May 17, the San Antonio Spurs won the first choice in the June draft and immediately announced their intention to choose David. "He's a terrific athlete," said the Spurs general manager. "When he gets with better players, he'll be even better."

Three days later, David and 1,021 of his classmates gathered in the Halsey Field House in Annapolis for graduation. One by one, thirty-six Navy companies walked to the podium. When it was his turn, David shook hands and received his diploma in mathematics and computer science from George Bush, then vice president and future president of the United States. When the last midshipman received his degree, the graduates all shouted "Beat Army!" and sailed their hats toward the sky.

Two weeks later, newly commissioned Ensign David Robinson received his orders. He was to report for duty on June 19 at Kings Bay Submarine Base in Georgia where he would serve as Assistant Resident Officer in Charge of Construction. For supervising the building of docks and service facilities for submarines, the Navy would pay him $315.23 a week.

On June 22, the San Antonio Spurs used their first pick in the NBA draft to select Ensign Robinson. They were willing to pay him millions of dollars now if he would agree to report for duty in Texas in two years to help them rebuild their basketball franchise.

David was in Washington, D.C., visiting with Vice President Bush at the White House and playing in a celebrity golf tournament with entertainer Bob Hope when he officially heard the news that the Spurs had drafted him.

"Will you sign with the Spurs?" the reporters wanted to know.

David pointed out that he already had a job. He told the reporters that he planned to visit San Antonio, meet people, look around, learn about the Spurs organization, and then make up his mind. The Spurs would need to convince him they were committed to improving their team, that the players were happy there, and that their fans would come out and support the team.

Later that summer, David and a bunch of other college All-Stars played for Team USA in the Pan American Games held that year in Indianapolis. The Americans expected to dominate. They'd won 47 games and lost only twice while winning the championship eight out of nine times since the Pan-Am games began.

When he didn't play particularly well until the semifinals against Puerto Rico, everyone was asking what was wrong with David Robinson. He felt he was in shape, but he admitted, "Kings Bay is a small town, and there is nowhere within an hour's drive that I can play competitive basketball."

In the final against Brazil, David got in foul trouble early. The Brazilians hung with the U.S. until David came back in and quickly fouled out of the contest. Then Brazil surged ahead to win the game and capture the gold medal. "This is far worse than losing to Duke in the NCAA tournament," David admitted to *The Washington Post*. "Our Pan American team was absolutely expected to win and didn't.... One of the worst feelings an athlete can have is knowing his teammates need him and not being able to do anything about it."

The bitter taste of defeat was washed away in September when David finally made his first visit to San Antonio. What an experience!

The Spurs spent $16,000 to charter a private jet to pick up David's parents and his brother, Chuck, along with David's two agents in Washington, D.C. Then they flew to Jacksonville, Florida, to pick up David.

When they landed in San Antonio, seven hundred screaming fans met the plane. Chuck Robinson, who looks a lot like his older brother but is several inches shorter, stepped out of the plane first. The crowd cheered wildly — though some of them must have been thinking seven feet wasn't nearly as tall as they thought it was. They were quickly reassured, however, when David ducked his head and stepped through the plane's door behind his brother.

A number of dignitaries made presentations. David said a few words to the crowd as many of them chanted "David! David! David!" and waved signs with messages such as "Say yes! David" and "Pretty Please?" After a short press conference, the entire family was whisked away to the city's nicest hotel, where they were given suites with bedrooms, dining rooms, and even living rooms with fireplaces.

Some Spurs players and officials took the Robinsons to a fancy dinner. The next morning the Spurs' bosses and the mayor took them on a helicopter tour of the city, and then to the city's most prestigious country club for lunch and a round of golf. That night, David and his family enjoyed another elegant dinner at a French restaurant and a boat ride along the city's famous River Walk.

The following day, David met with the Spurs' officials one more time. He made no promises. But he told everyone how great it felt to be wanted and how impressed he was with the city. "I just need some time to mull over my decision," he told them.

Some people figured David would hold out until he could sign with the Lakers or the Celtics. But after just a few weeks, he gave his agents permission to see what kind of contract San Antonio had in mind. When he heard their offer, he told his friend and old roommate Hootie Liebert, "They have done everything to make me happy. They have been honest and fair. How can I turn them down?"

On November 6, 1987, David and his parents flew to San Antonio, where five hundred fans watched and cheered as he signed his contract at the HemisFair Arena. The contract made David the highest paid athlete in team sports — $26 million for eight years, plus $2 million immediately just for signing.

Now David and the city of San Antonio had to be content to wait for his professional basketball career to begin — after he finished his obligation to the Navy. In the meantime, David confessed to a *Washington Post* reporter that, "I'm living in two different worlds right now. One world I rule. It's all there on a silver platter for me. People want to give me an incredible amount of money to play a game — something I enjoy. That boggles my mind.

"In the other world, I'm at the bottom of the totem pole. I might be asked to run out and get coffee for people. The whole situation is teaching me a lot. I'm learning about power and restraint."

Later he would add, "I would go to NBA things — go

Edwards Dibaia/AP Photo

As part of the U.S. basketball team during the 1988 Summer Olympics in Seoul, Korea, David helps block a 2-point shot by China's Fengwu San. The U.S. won 108–57.

to the All-Star game, for instance, where everyone was treated special—then come back to the base, where guys were going to the supermarket with their families, working jobs, doing all the normal things people do. I had a foot in both worlds."

"Tell me one thing," David would say to his friends after he came back from one of his outings in the world of celebrity. "Tell me if I ever change, if my head ever starts to get bigger."

But David got a dose of humility the next year when he went to the Olympic trials. His job hadn't given him much time to work out, and for almost a year he'd had no chance to compete against top-notch basketball players. David's skills were so rusty that people again wondered what was wrong with him.

When he averaged only 12.8 points and 6.8 rebounds a game during the Olympics themselves, and the coach failed to play him in the deciding minutes of the semifinal loss to the Soviet Union, more people began to question both David's skills and his commitment to basketball. Would he even be able to play at the professional level after another year away from the game?

David had his own doubts. For a long time, he blamed himself for his U.S. team ending up with a bronze rather than a gold medal.

Would he disappoint the people in San Antonio, too?

Chapter 13

Fame and Fortune

On May 19, 1989, the United States Navy gave Lieutenant (Junior Grade) David Robinson his official discharge from active duty. The time had finally come to begin his professional basketball career. People remembered his disappointing performances in the Pan American and Olympic games. "If he couldn't lead his American teams to victories in competitions that the U.S. had traditionally dominated," they asked, "how could he be expected to succeed in the NBA against the best competition in the world?"

David heard the comments and remembered his own bitter disappointment against international competition. He became even more determined to fulfill his potential and reward the faith that the San Antonio Spurs had shown in him.

With no more college classes to attend and no other

job to take his time, David Robinson was, for the first time in his life, ready to concentrate all of his attention and energy on basketball. How good could he be? After two years of waiting and wondering, he was ready to find out.

David began to get into shape and tune up his game. Then he silenced some of the critics by dominating the summer pro leagues in Texas and Southern California. He wowed his teammates and coaches during training camp and more than held his own in the pre-season exhibition games against other NBA teams.

Anticipation began to build. David Robinson became the talk of the town in San Antonio, Texas. In the two years since the Spurs signed him, the team had won 52 games and lost 112. They had just changed owners, and only three players were back from the previous year's team. Clearly, everyone was counting on David Robinson to turn the tide for the Spurs franchise and transform the image of professional sports in the city.

November 4, 1989, finally arrived. "The Admiral" would make his NBA debut against the Los Angeles Lakers.

David felt the pressure. He was so nervous that he threw up in the locker room before the game. But soon after the tip-off, David took a pass in the lane, leaped into the air with his back to the basket, and slam-dunked the ball over his head. The crowd roared.

David led his team by scoring 23 points and hauling down a game-high of 17 rebounds to propel the once-hapless Spurs to a 106–98 victory over the Lakers. His

Rogers Photo Archive/Getty Images

David played a hard game during his first NBA year, as seen here against the New Jersey Nets.

performance prompted a defeated Magic Johnson to say after the game, "Some rookies are never really rookies. Robinson is one of them."

With the Admiral in command, the Spurs won 12 of their first 17 games. The same experts who'd wondered how he would play after two years away from the game called him one of the premier centers in the

NBA—right up there with Patrick Ewing and Hakeem Olajuwon. Some commentators were predicting, "He's going to be the best center to ever play the game." His own coach, Larry Brown, called him "the best player of that size I've ever seen."

The longer the season went on, the bigger the impression David Robinson made. He was named to the All-Star game and was a unanimous pick for NBA Rookie of the Year while averaging 24.3 points, 12.0 rebounds, and 3.9 blocks a game. The 1989–90 Spurs won 35 more games than they had the previous year—the biggest one-year turnaround in league history. And in the NBA's post-season playoffs, David led his team to the Western Conference semi-finals.

In David's second year as a pro, the NBA reported more Robinson merchandise sold than for any other player except Michael Jordan. In one year, he'd become a superstar with a national following.

David was the only NBA player to place in the top ten in four statistical categories. The top vote-getter for the West All-Star Team, he was also named All-NBA First Team, All-NBA Defensive Team, and came in third in the voting for Most Valuable Player behind Michael Jordan and Magic Johnson. As a team, the Spurs won their division in the regular season, but disappointed their fans by losing to Golden State in the first round of the playoffs.

Very few people blamed David. He obviously did more than his part for the Spurs and established himself as one of the best players in the history of the game.

Andrew D. Bernstein/Getty Images

NBA Commissioner David Stern presents the Rookie of the Year award to David at the Alamodome in San Antonio, Texas, in 1990.

David had more money, fame, and success than he'd ever dreamed. He was young, smart, good looking, and incredibly rich. He had five fancy cars and two beautiful homes. He went out with gorgeous women. People were always telling him how great he was. Everyone he met seemed to want to do something for him.

When his brother, Chuck, came to visit David, he couldn't believe his brother's lifestyle. "This is awesome," he told David. "You've got it made."

Looking back, David admits his brother was right. "My first year in the NBA, everything was going my way. I was playing well; I was All-NBA team. I had a lot of endorsements ... everything you can think of. I had the house, the money, the fans, but I wasn't at peace."

Despite all he had, his life just didn't seem satisfying. David couldn't help feeling something was wrong. Yet he didn't understand what.

"Success was like cotton candy. It tastes great when you first put it in your mouth, but it dissolves real quick," David says. "I'd gotten a lot of success quickly, made a lot of money, had all the nice toys I wanted, but it didn't make me happy. There was no real substance to it. It was neat, but it just dissolved away to nothing. You wake up in the morning, and you still have to look at yourself in the mirror and wonder what kind of man you're going to be."

The truth was, fame and fortune had already begun to change David. Other people still saw him as a great guy and a wonderful role model. But he says, "When I looked at myself, I didn't like the person I was becoming. I felt I was so important. I had a selfishness and an arrogance. If I was thirty minutes late, I'd think, *It doesn't matter, because they can't start without me. I'm the one who counts.* I found myself doing that more and more.

"I was unsettled—happy one day, sad the next. If the press wrote a critical article about me, I'd be down. If everyone was patting me on the back, I'd feel great." He was taking his cues from everyone else's opinion of him and that was always changing. He knew he needed something else on which to base his feelings—and his life.

During the 1990–91 season, a man named Greg Ball from the organization Champions for Christ approached David one day after a Spurs' practice. He said he was a minister and had been praying especially for him. As soon as David heard Greg's words, he apologized, "Oh, I gotta go. Maybe we can talk another time."

In June of 1991, David saw Greg Ball again and agreed to give him a few minutes of his time. They went to David's home, and after a little casual conversation, Greg asked, "David, do you love God?"

"Of course I love God," David replied, surprised by the question.

"How much time do you spend praying?"

"Every once in a while. Before I eat. Sometimes before I go to bed."

"How much time do you spend reading the Bible?" Greg asked.

"I've got one around here somewhere," David replied, feeling a little uneasy. "I just don't understand very much of it."

Greg Ball pressed on, "When you love someone, don't you usually take time to get to know them?"

"Sure," David agreed. He didn't say it, but he was thinking, *But God isn't a real person.*

"The Old Testament says to set aside one day a week to honor God," Greg was saying. "When was the last time you spent one day, not one day a week, but just one day praising God and thanking him for what you have?"

"That's when the Lord grabbed me. He showed me how much he had loved me all this time, and how I hadn't responded to his love," David remembers. And he finally understood why he'd been feeling so uneasy. The moment he heard Greg Ball's question, David thought, *I've never given God a day to pray and thank him! I really have been acting like a spoiled brat. Everything has been about me, me, me. How much money can I make? My life is all about David's praise, David's glory. I play basketball to hear everybody cheering me and have them pat me on the back. I've never stopped to honor God or think about all he has given me.*

David suddenly felt so ashamed he began to cry, and he couldn't stop. He cried all afternoon. He realized God was real, and that God had sent Greg Ball to deliver this message. All the material things he had were like cotton candy—nothing to them. They couldn't do anything to fill up his empty soul.

David realized, "Without God, I have nothing. I am nothing." Admitting that, he says, "pushed me over the edge and helped me give my life to Jesus."

So he closed his eyes and prayed, telling God, "You've blessed me, given me so much, everything I have, and I've never honored you, never thanked you. I've been like a spoiled kid in the house. You blessing me, Lord, and me running around doing what I want to do."

How sorry he was for the ungrateful way he'd been acting and living.

"Everything you've given me," David promised God, "I'm giving back to you today. From here on, Lord, everything I have is yours. Where you want me to go, I'll go; whatever you want me to say, I'll say. Lord let me walk with you, let me hold your hand. Let me be your child."

David knew his life changed forever that afternoon. But he wasn't sure what to do next. Greg Ball handed him a Bible and told him it was "the manual for life."

David was an engineer—a tinkerer who always wanted to know how things worked. He actually read manuals for fun just to learn how some computer or new software worked. *The Bible was a manual? For life? No kidding!* he thought.

"The very next day," according to David, "God gave me this incredible hunger for his Word. I would get in my Bible and read—for hours at a time. I was so hungry to know who God was. Before that I had known almost nothing about God. Now as I read the Bible, the Word just became alive to me. It began to transform me as I got to know God, and to love him as my father."

Greg Ball says David was "like a sponge." He got so excited about what he was learning that he called his brother to tell him he was reading the Bible and how it was changing him!

"David," Chuck told him, "you're scaring me!"

But the truth of what he was feeling and learning really came home to him a few days later. David watched on television as the Bulls celebrated their first world championship. He says, "I saw Michael Jordan hugging that trophy, and I remember thinking, *Wow! I've always wanted to be like Mike, right? Win the championship, be the best player in the game. I want all the stuff he has.* But as I watched him kiss that trophy, I thought, *That's great right now. But in six months people will be telling him, 'Magic has five of those. You only have one.'*

"And it hit me again. Pursuing success is like chasing your tail. You can never win. Proving yourself to others is like trying to catch the wind. No matter what you do, someone always raises the bar. Or they start tearing you down. And I realized if that's where I was going, I was in a lot of trouble. That's a road to nowhere. It's like running after a rainbow. The world's idea of success is never going to fulfill me. There really has to be another way."

David was now sure he'd finally found it.

Chapter 14

A New Man

"I was reading the Bible three and four hours a day," David says. "And I couldn't believe how much I was learning. The words just seemed to jump off the page at me. I had no idea all that wisdom was in there. It was like the Lord speaking to me. It was so clear all of a sudden."

David quickly realized his new commitment to God meant he would be a new man. But he never imagined all the ways his new faith would change his life.

Most people who had known David Robinson hadn't seen any reason for him to change. He was one of the finest role models in sports—not just an athlete but a scholar, a good citizen, an officer, and a gentleman. He always stood ramrod straight throughout the playing of the national anthem. He was so squeaky clean he didn't even drink or smoke. He regularly spoke at school assemblies telling kids to stay in school and off of drugs.

The Admiral was truly admirable. What was there not to like? When people first heard that he'd become a born-again Christian, many people wondered why in the world David thought he needed to change.

"But they only saw me from the world's perspective," David says. "And the world doesn't have very high standards to live up to. We all can compare ourselves to someone we think is worse than we are and decide we're pretty good people. I did that." Plus David had a lot of other people telling him what a good person he was. So he says he had to understand that he didn't come close to measuring up to God's standard. He knew he needed Christ's presence and help in his life.

David says that one of the Bible passages he found most helpful is from the Gospel of Luke's account of Jesus asking, "Can the blind lead the blind? Will they not both fall into the pit?" (6:39). David says it hit him: "I am a blind man. How can I encourage someone else when I don't know where I'm going myself? I was only beginning to see things from God's perspective. I finally had something to give somebody else.

"I remembered all those times I'd gone to high schools to tell kids to Say NO! to drugs. Now I realized I hadn't been giving the kids anything real. Maybe they were impressed with me for a few moments, but I could never change their lives. However, if I could give them Christ, he could change their lives through and through. So it was a great feeling to know that from now on when I shared with people, it wasn't just me anymore. God would work through me. And he could reach and change peoples' hearts."

And God did indeed work through David Robinson — starting at a school in one of the poorest neighborhoods in San Antonio.

The first time David Robinson walked into their classroom, all the fifth graders at Gates Elementary School in San Antonio, Texas, looked up. Way up!

Of course, they had known he was tall. You can't play center for the San Antonio Spurs and be an NBA All-Star without being a very big man. But watching professional basketball players running back and forth on a TV screen, even if it's a large screen, doesn't really prepare you for having a seven-foot, one-inch giant stand over your desk at school.

The year was 1991. And one of the greatest basketball players in the world was paying a visit to an elementary school on San Antonio's Eastside. Why? His mother asked him to.

Although the neighborhood was just a few blocks from one of the city's most popular tourist attractions, the ritzy River Walk, the deserted and run-down buildings of the Eastside had a profound impact on the athlete. It seemed to be a place where dreams too often die. "A lot of kids were getting into drugs and crime," David said. "You grow up in that circle, and that's all you see." He couldn't get over the fact that many kids never got past the ten- to fifteen-block area where they grew up.

Freda Robinson, David's mother, attended and taught Sunday school at an Eastside church. She knew some of the teachers, and she'd met many of the African-American and Hispanic students enrolled at Gates Elementary. She believed the kids she'd encountered needed someone to look up to—someone like her son.

Mrs. Robinson believed the Eastside fifth graders she'd met had a lot of potential. But because most of them were growing up in poor families—many with unhappy or tragic backgrounds—the odds were stacked against them. She knew the majority of Gates Elementary students would eventually drop out of school. Perhaps she could find a way to encourage them to strive for their potential. That's when she decided to propose a radical idea to her son.

"Mom always had a heart for the community and for those kids," David says. "So she came to me and said, 'I've got a great idea that could really make a difference in kids' lives.' I'd always believed in the value of education, and after I met those kids I thought, *This really could work!* Now's the time to get kids started thinking about their futures. If in fifth grade kids believe it really is possible that they could go to college someday, they could begin planning and aiming for that goal. We just need to help them realize the opportunity will be there."

So what was this idea designed to inspire kids from San Antonio's Eastside? David told all ninety fifth graders at Gates Elementary that if they stayed in school and graduated from high school, he would give each graduate $2,000 to use for college or technical school training.

Those fifth graders could hardly believe it. Two thousand dollars apiece! David had to smile at their excitement. But he also told them in a rather stern tone, "You better take it seriously and say to yourself, 'Man, I want to make something out of myself.'" He told them that he was willing to set aside more than enough money to buy himself a nice Porsche. So he expected them to work hard.

David Robinson's scholarship promise was only part of the plan. Mrs. Robinson set up monthly progress meetings at the school to check up on the kids and talk to their teachers. David became a regular visitor at Gates Elementary, giving pep talks and advice to the students and personally getting to know the kids.

But one of the biggest surprises resulting from David's new faith involved his love life. He'd broken up with a young woman named Valerie Hoggatt a few months earlier. He'd been introduced to her by a friend when he was on temporary Navy duty in Southern California back in 1988. They dated a number of times, and when he'd returned to Kings Bay (GA) Naval Submarine Base, their relationship continued long distance. She came to see him. He visited her. And Valerie became his steady girlfriend.

But she was David's ex-girlfriend by the time he'd committed his life to God. "I had told Valerie that she loved me too much," David says. "That I could never have the love for her, the passion for her, that she had for me. And I needed to find someone I could love as much as she loved me."

However, now as David read his Bible and prayed for God to give him direction in life, he kept thinking about

Valerie. *How could he have said what he said to her?* It was another area of his life where he'd been incredibly selfish. She'd been so loving toward him, and he hadn't even tried to love her the same way.

David called Valerie and told her that he had given his life to God and been reading the Bible. She told him that she also had been studying the Bible and growing closer to the Lord. "We got back together," David says. "We read the Bible together. She was the same sweet, wonderful person she had been before. I just hadn't been paying attention. Our whole relationship was different now that God was in it."

Three months later, David stunned Valerie when he asked her to marry him. She said yes, and they were married in December 1991 at Tired Stone Baptist Church in San Antonio. The national media reported on the wedding from outside the church. Only family, a few friends, and a number of David's teammates witnessed the private ceremony.

Everyone was happy for the new couple. David's coach even speculated that having a wife to go home to might help stabilize the personal life of his star and perhaps even make him a better basketball player. But some observers worried and openly wondered if David's new faith might have an opposite effect.

One criticism about David through the years was that he didn't have that competitive nature—the killer instinct needed to win a championship. "He's too thoughtful, too bright, and he has too many other interests to devote himself totally to basketball," people would say.

Andrew D. Bernstein/Getty Images

David joined the original Olympic Dream Team that included such basketball greats as Michael Jordan, Magic Johnson, Larry Bird, Charles Barkley, and Patrick Ewing. They captured the gold medal in the Barcelona Summer Games in 1992.

No one ever questioned his physical skills, but some people wondered about his commitment to the game. Now many expected David's new faith to weaken his game by making him "soft." They thought God might be yet another interest that would take away from his commitment to competitive basketball.

They need not have worried. As outstanding as David had been in his first two years as a professional, he continued to improve. He had another All-NBA season in 1991–92. Unfortunately, he tore a ligament in his hand in the spring, needed surgery, and had to sit and watch his teammates be eliminated in the first round of the playoffs. He did recover in time to join the rest of the original Olympic Dream Team that included such basketball greats as Michael Jordan, Magic Johnson, Larry Bird, Charles Barkley, and Patrick Ewing, and they captured the gold medal in the Barcelona Summer Games.

Chapter 15

Win Some, Lose Some

The 1992–93 Spurs went through turmoil when their new coach resigned suddenly after a disappointing start. The team rallied under yet another coach, John Lucas. David again put in an All-Star season and led an injury-plagued team to the playoffs where they lost again. Then in 1994, David won the NBA scoring title, barely edging out Shaquille O'Neal, by racking up an amazing 71 points against the Los Angeles Clippers in his final game of the 1993-94 regular season.

No one who participated in or watched that remarkable game will ever forget it. David started fast against the Clippers by scoring the Spurs' first 18 points of the game. None of his teammates even scored until there was 23 seconds left in the first quarter.

"It was unbelievable," David told reporters after the game. "My team has been behind me the whole year.

They always push me to do a lot of individual things. As a leader, I just try to win games, but tonight they really wanted me to shoot it. When the game started, they were looking for me almost every time down the court."

His scoring pace slowed in the second quarter when he added only six more points to his total. But David bounced back with 19 in the third quarter and an astounding 28 more in a monster fourth quarter—including seven in the final 59 seconds of the game.

Afterwards some critics complained that the achievement was somehow tainted because David's coach left him in long after the outcome of the game had been decided for the victorious Spurs. But Coach John Lucas, who actually yelled at David to quit passing and shoot the ball, explained his thinking to reporters after the game: "Everybody wanted him to get it, and everybody was mad that he was passing some shots up. David deserves it. Sometimes I have to push David to become selfish."

Actually saying "everybody" wanted David to win the scoring title was a slight exaggeration. Some of the Clippers' players cursed and taunted David out on the floor, saying, "You're not going to get it. You'll never get it!"

As David remembers his opponents in that game, he says, "I had a lot of work going after those points. The Clippers really didn't want me to have the scoring title; they were bumping and grinding and double-teaming me. That's the hardest I'd ever had to work for some points."

Even so, the Los Angeles fans got behind David's scoring title chase, cheering wildly each time he scored in the final quarter, while actually booing their own team when the Clippers tried to slow him down by holding the ball at the end of the game. And anyone who thought David's achievement wasn't legitimate only had to look at his statistics for the game. He hit 26 of his 41 shots from the field, including one of two three-pointers. He also hit 18 of 25 free throws—his 18 foul shots tying a team record, and his 25 foul-shot attempts breaking a team record. (The Clippers really did all they could to stop him.) And yet, on top of all that scoring, David grabbed 10 rebounds, dished out 5 assists to his teammates, and played his trademark-tough defense in the lane—blocking multiple shots by the Clippers.

Asked to explain his thoughts and feelings after what was a truly historic NBA game, David told reporters when he looked up at the scoreboard and finally realized what he'd done, "I said, '71 points. Oh, my goodness!'

"I have never thought about a lot of personal stuff. To me, that just comes along with winning. I don't know where to rank this right now. I've got to sit around and kind of let it settle in." And then he added, "I'm really fortunate to have scored over 70 points. I don't really have that many opportunities to do something like this." With a smile he finally admitted, "It was fun. I had a great time!"

Asked later about the role his faith played in his career, David told *Sports Illustrated* that as a Christian, he's come to realize that playing basketball was a God-given gift— and it was his duty to make the most of that gift.

"I'm not playing for the fans or the money," he told the magazine, "but to honor God. Every night I get out there and try to honor him and play great."

David also believed that the better he played, the more people would listen to him, and the greater his opportunity would be to influence others for Christ.

His new, higher motivation obviously worked. His coach John Lucas called David "the best basketball player in the game—there has never been another player like him."

The coach of the rival Seattle Supersonics, George Karl, said about the improvement, "This is a different David Robinson than we've seen in the past. He's a much more dangerous player. I've always said the man, if he would ever commit to winning, would be as scary as anybody in the league."

David led his team to a fantastic 60–22 record in the regular 1994–95 season. And just before the opening game of the NBA playoff series against Hakeem Olajuwon and the Houston Rockets, the announcement was made that David had won the year's Most Valuable Player (MVP) award.

But neither the season record, the MVP trophy, nor David's strong personal performance made any difference. Hakeem played a better playoff series than David did, and Houston won the Western Conference Finals in six games.

David, his teammates, and the San Antonio fans had

Scott Cunningham/Getty Images

NBA Commissioner David Stern (l) and Spurs' head coach Bob Hill
(r) present David with the MVP award during the 1995 season.

been so convinced this was the Spurs' year. "It felt like
falling off a cliff," David admitted, "to go from something so high to something so low in such a short time. I
don't think there's any worse feeling for an athlete than
to feel inadequate. These are the times when you really
have to love the game, when you realize you were six
games away from a title, and now you have to start all
over again."

A successful 1995–96 season also ended for David without the long-sought NBA championship. But that disappointment was eased a bit later in the summer when David and his U.S. teammates won the gold medal in the Atlanta Olympic Games. David became the first American male basketball player to enjoy the honor of competing in three Olympics.

And in 1996, the National Basketball Association honored the Admiral by naming David one of the 50 Greatest Players in NBA History.

Despite the highs and lows, the great honors and the deep disappointments of 1996, the following season of 1996–97 proved to be perhaps the most difficult and frustrating season in David's career. After winning a franchise-high 62 games in 1994–95 and following that with 59 victories in 1995–96, expectations were higher than ever before for the Spurs. But injuries to several key players shattered any championship dreams.

David himself missed the beginning of the season with back problems. Then after playing only half the minutes in just six games, he broke his foot and was out for the remainder of the season.

The injuries that David suffered that season had some advantages. Not having to travel all season with his team enabled David to spend more time at home with his family. At the time he and Valerie had two young boys—David Jr. and Corey. Their son Justin would be born a year later. David says the experience taught him that fatherhood is, by far, a tougher and more important job than being a professional basketball player.

David and his U.S. teammates won the gold medal in the 1996 Atlanta Olympic Games.

"The responsibility is huge," he says. "You realize that you're impacting their lives. You try to set a standard. I really take it very seriously. It's fun. But it's also challenging." And when it comes to basketball versus fatherhood, he says his kids are his higher priority.

Without David, the Spurs won only twenty games that 1996-97 basketball season and missed the playoffs for the first time since he joined the team. David began to wonder about his chances of ever winning an NBA title.

Chapter 16

Twin Towers

Another good thing resulted from San Antonio's terrible season record in the 1996–97 year. The Spurs were given a place in the draft lottery—and they struck gold. After winning the number one pick in the 1997 NBA draft, the Spurs landed super-prospect Tim Duncan, a multi-talented, seven-foot, All-American out of Wake Forest University.

Some observers wondered how David would react to sharing the Spurs' stage with the multi-talented new-comer. A lot of veteran stars might have been jealous or sulked, but not the Admiral. Soon after Duncan signed his contract, David invited the rookie to join him at his summer home in Colorado.

For almost two weeks, David and his new teammate ran conditioning drills up and down Aspen Mountain. Then they practiced together in a local high school gym.

David was impressed not only with Duncan's talent, but also his willingness to work and learn. David let his new friend know he wanted to do everything possible to help him be and do his best.

That was an incredibly unselfish attitude on David's part. After all, David was one of the league's biggest, most-recognized stars and his own team's long-established leader. He already had a Most Valuable Player trophy on a shelf at home, made seven trips to the All-Star game, and had two Olympic gold medals. He'd also led the NBA in scoring and in blocked shots and had been named the league's defensive player of the year.

Yet by Duncan's second season, he was San Antonio's top scorer. Loyal, long-time Spurs' fans excitedly expected their powerhouse team to make the deepest play-off run in franchise history.

And through it all, David Robinson was a willing accomplice in Tim Duncan's ascension to stardom in San Antonio. "If we can win games, everybody's going to be happy," David said. "For me, when Tim came, the very first thing I told him was, 'I'm going to put you in position where you can succeed. Period. That's it. If you're a better scorer than me, I'll put you down on the block, so you can score. I don't care. I can do other things.' "

Together, these two friends and teammates turned the Spurs fortunes around. San Antonio's record in Tim's first season was an even bigger improvement over the previous year than the record-setting turnaround back in David's rookie season.

Opponents who managed to slow down one of the

"twin towers" seldom stopped the other. David concentrated more on defense and distributing the scoring. And for the first complete season since he joined the team, he wasn't his team's leading scorer or rebounder. Duncan edged him out in both categories. Tim won Rookie of the Year honors and drew tremendous acclaim as the greatest impact player to join the league since Shaquille O'Neal.

In the meantime, some experts questioned whether David's reduced stats were an indication that his skills were deteriorating with age. Wiser observers praised him for his selflessness in assisting Tim's success. They understood that the team was stronger than ever because of David's willingness to take a different, more specialized, and perhaps "lesser" role.

David now says he probably got too much credit for accepting a "reduced" role because it seemed to him like a no-brainer. "My skills always lent themselves to being a cleanup man, playing defense, disrupting a game, and making things happen," he says. "Tim's talents make him the perfect go-to guy—he has all the hook shots and other nice moves."

What few people realized was how David's selfless attitude was such a powerful example of Jesus' teaching. Not just the Golden Rule ("Do unto others as you would have them do unto you"), but also the idea that true greatness comes from putting the interests of others ahead of your own. (See Matthew 23:12 and Mark 9:35.)

Still, David admits it's not always easy to share the glory. "Sure," he says, "it's great to be 'The Man'—getting all the attention and the accolades when you win. But we became a better team with the credit and the glory shared.

"I was frustrated for ten years without a championship—always trying to figure out what more I could do. It served as an important life lesson to realize I couldn't do that by myself either."

Prior to the 1998–99 season, the NBA owners and league commissioner David Stern locked out the NBA Players' Association to force negotiations on a new collective bargaining agreement. This lockout lasted for 202 days, well into the regular NBA season, before an agreement was finally reached. After playing a shortened 50-game season, the Spurs finished with an NBA-best record of 37–13, earning them home-court advantage through the post-season.

San Antonio blitzed through the first three rounds of the NBA playoffs. First they beat the Minnesota Timberwolves, next the Los Angeles Lakers, and then the Portland Trail Blazers. Altogether they won eleven games and lost only one.

In the NBA finals, the combination of Robinson at center and Tim Duncan at power forward proved overpowering. The Spurs trounced the underdog New York Knicks after just five games in the best-of-seven series to become the NBA champions for the very first time. Duncan won the personal honor of being named the Finals' Most Valuable Player.

The buzzer sounded at the end of the last game with the usual championship post-game celebration—everyone running around hugging everyone else. But David says, "I just felt dazed. My mind was saying, *Is it over?* One minute you're still climbing, and the next minute everything you've been working for is right there. The suddenness of it can throw you for a loop. Yes, it was a thrill. But after ten years in the NBA, all my emotion wasn't going to come out in one moment.

"I'm sure some of my teammates had a pretty wild party after we won that championship game," David recalls. But he'd promised David Jr. he could sleep next to Dad if the Spurs won game five, and the boy had actually cried when San Antonio fell behind in the second half. So how did the Spurs' star center celebrate his team's last-minute victory? He hurried back to his New York hotel room, climbed into bed beside his six-year-old son, and went to sleep.

Later as David reflected on his feelings about finally achieving the world championship, he again credited his faith. He said being a Christian not only helped motivate him, but also helped him deal with the ego and pride issues of playing alongside a great player like Tim Duncan.

David admitted, "I can't deny it felt weird to see Tim standing on the podium with the Finals MVP trophy. I was thinking, *Man, never have I come to the end of a tournament and not been the one holding up that trophy.* It was hard. But I thought about the Bible story of David and Goliath. David helped King Saul win the battle, but the king wasn't happy because he had killed thousands of the enemy while David had killed tens of thousands. So

King Saul couldn't enjoy the victory. He was too worried about David getting more credit than he was. I'm blessed that God gave me the ability to enjoy the victory. So Tim killed the tens of thousands. That's great. I can be happy for him."

David wasn't caught up with the hardware, however. When photographers wanted a picture of him kissing the championship trophy, he refused saying, "I'm not kissing anything that doesn't kiss me back."

He explains, "Everybody thinks the trophy and the ring are the ultimate goals. But as meaningful and valuable as they are, they are just things. They'll wind up on a shelf somewhere."

"The journey, the experience of winning will be in my heart forever," David says about the momentous event. And he soon began dreaming of winning another championship.

But he, his teammates, and their city were all deeply disappointed when the Spurs were eliminated from the playoffs in the 1999–2000 and 2000–01 seasons. David helped convince (he laughingly claims he made a special flight home from Hawaii and "got down on my knees to beg") Tim Duncan to sign a new contract with the team in 2000, committing himself to stay in San Antonio. Then in 2001, David signed one last Spurs contract of his own for millions less than he might have gotten as a free agent going to some team in a bigger city like Chicago, Los Angeles, or New York.

David did so hoping for another shot at a championship with Tim Duncan and the Spurs. More importantly,

Eric Gray/AP Photo

After beating the New Jersey Nets 88-77 in game 6 of the NBA
finals to win the championship in 2003, David holds up the
championship trophy while Tim Duncan holds up the MVP trophy.
This was David's last NBA game.

he wanted to finish out his professional basketball career in the city that was now his home—where he learned that there are more important things in life than basketball and where he believed God had more for him to do.

Chapter 17

True Success

During his years in San Antonio, David had watched the students at Gates Elementary who were fifth graders in 1991 as they moved on to middle school and then high school. David, his wife, Valerie, and his mother, Freda, stayed in touch with them. In addition to the monthly progress meetings, they had big annual get-togethers for the kids and sometimes their families—like cookouts at David's parents' house and outings to a major amusement park.

In 1998, about fifty of those kids from Gates Elementary received their high school diplomas. David attended the graduation ceremony for twenty-five of them at Sam Houston High in San Antonio. "People say I've given them this, but really these kids have given me a lot more," David said. "I went to that graduation, and I felt like a dad to twenty-five kids. How cool is that?"

There is no way of knowing how many of those kids would have stayed in school if, back in 1991, David Robinson had not made them that promise of tuition money for college if they graduated. But if you talk to them today, student after student will tell you that the San Antonio Spurs' MVP center has also been a "most valuable player" in their lives.

One of the students, Homer Adams III, earned his undergraduate degree from Tuskegee Institute, a Masters in genomics from Washington State University, and a Ph.D. in breast cancer research at the University of Medicine and Dentistry of New Jersey.

"Because of David, I feel an obligation to push, to keep going, to do more," he says. And that *more* includes mentoring young people. "I'm anxious to get to the point where I can give back—time-wise and money—to give kids motivation to pursue their dreams."

Jeffrey Ledet, another of the Gates students, does not remember much about David's stay-in-school speech. "I was just amazed at how tall he was," Jeffrey said. But David's program required the students to meet with a mentor twice a month. With the encouragement of his mentor and support from David, Jeffrey entered his school's eighth-grade science fair and came in third place. Then Jeffrey went on to get a Bachelor of Science degree in engineering and a Masters in business administration.

According to Jeffrey, one of the gifts David gave all his Gates classmates was a whole new perspective on life. "We learned that there's a bigger world outside of what we knew from the east side of San Antonio."

David not only stayed involved with that group of kids from Gates Elementary, he and Valerie also started and continue to fund the David Robinson Foundation to channel their giving around the city.

Some of the programs the David Robinson Foundation sponsored are Neighborhood Students, a mentoring program for local students; Feed My Sheep, which provided food to organizations that feed the hungry; and The Ruth Project, which offered diapers and baby food to needy families with infants.

Through the Mister Robinson's Neighborhood of Achievers program, the David Robinson Foundation purchased 50 (David's jersey number) tickets to each Spurs home game—41 games each year—to be given to students in recognition of accomplishments of all kinds.

David knew that he couldn't personally provide scholarships and encouragement for all the needy children in San Antonio in the same way he had for the Gates Elementary students. So he came up with what he believed could become a better, long-range strategy. In 1997, he and Valerie announced they were donating $5 million to help build a private Christian school on the southeast side of San Antonio. Their contribution is the largest single monetary gift in history given by a sports star.

The Carver Academy (TCA) is named after the famous African-American scientist George Washington

Andrew D. Bernstein/NBAE via Getty Images

David Robinson #50, along with Malik Rose #31, NBA Commissioner David Stern, and members of the San Antonio Spurs organization cut the ribbon to the Spurs Reading and Learning Center at the Carver Academy on June 5, 2003 in San Antonio, Texas.

Carver and helps provide disadvantaged children with a quality education that their families could not otherwise afford. TCA opened on September 17, 2001, on a 5-acre inner-city campus with 60 students.

Since the start of the school, David and his wife, Valerie, have given over $10 million of their own money to The Carver Academy. And David not only serves as chairman of their board. He also finds time to show up at school to talk to students and to be a leader in development and raising endowment funds for the school.

"I get a chance to come over here and be the biggest cheerleader for these kids they will ever see. And I'm here for moral support and encouragement," David has said. "My career as a sports figure has been exciting, but its main purpose is to provide a platform for me to impact people's lives in a positive way."

In spite of David and Valerie's donation to the school, the walls at The Carver Academy boast no pictures of David nor plaques honoring him or his basketball career—at David's insistence.

The Robinsons see TCA not as a way for them to promote themselves, but "to build a foundation for future generations. We want to make these children the heroes of tomorrow by teaching them principles of integrity, discipline, and faith," explains David. "From the beginning, The Carver Academy students have performed extremely well. They take the Stanford Achievement Test, a common test for schools across the nation. And they've scored consistently in the top 25 percent of all schools tested.

"The quality of education at The Carver Academy is phenomenal. We expose the kids to a tremendous balance of culture," David says. "We have wonderful partnerships with the Institute of Texan Cultures, the Japan America Society, the Jewish Community Center, and the Carver Cultural Center. Our children are not only going to learn culture from books; they're going to live it."

TCA teaches its students Spanish, German, and Japanese. Its state-of-the-art engineering program allows elementary school students to design robots and deliver television news in a broadcast studio. Carver students are getting one of the best educations possible.

The mission of The Carver Academy, as David goes on to explain, "is to offer elementary-age children a challenging academic program featuring small classes, leadership opportunities, and a nurturing, family-like environment based upon the foundation of Judeo-Christian Scripture. Graduates of TCA will be prepared for success in the nation's most competitive high schools and will display the highest levels of leadership, discipline, initiative, and integrity."

Chapter 18

The End of a Fourteen-Year NBA Career

David and the Spurs began the 1999-2000 NBA season with high hopes of successfully defending the team's long-awaited first championship. But any hopes of repeating that feat ended when Tim Duncan suffered a season-ending knee injury that required surgery and kept him out of the playoffs. San Antonio lost to the Phoenix Suns in the opening round.

After David persuaded his teammate to re-sign with the Spurs, the Robinson/Duncan duo enabled San Antonio to once again compile the NBA's best overall record for the 2000–01 regular season. They made the playoffs for the eleventh time in David's twelve years on the team. But the Los Angeles Lakers cut the season short by downing the Spurs in the Western Conference finals.

The Spurs delivered yet another strong performance in the 2001–02 campaign, during which Tim Duncan won the league's MVP award. David also made Spurs history that year. First, he became the team's all-time scoring leader, surpassing Hall-of-Famer George Gervin. And later in the season, David became the twenty-seventh NBA player of all-time (and tenth center) to score 20,000 career points.

But even though he continued to reach significant personal career milestones, when the Lakers eliminated the Spurs again in the 2002 playoffs, 37-year-old David Robinson came to the conclusion that his role with the Spurs was coming to an end. He informed team management that he had decided the upcoming 2002–03 season would be his last. And the Spurs, their fans, and the entire city of San Antonio began preparing for the end of an era.

Tim Duncan, now a five-year veteran, had already assumed a big part of the on-floor leadership of the team. And the Spurs had continued to change and improve. They added 19-year-old French phenom Tony Parker to the team's starting lineup as point guard during the 2001–02 season. Going into David's last season, San Antonio signed the promising shooting-guard and Argentinian-Italian star Manu Ginobili as Parker's new backcourt partner.

This new blood not only internationalized the Spurs fan base, but it also energized the veteran San Antonio club and its fans. People flocked to see their exciting young Spurs and their veteran center play his last season, and their first, in the city's swank, new basketball arena, the SBC Center.

Many observers noted the surprisingly smooth integration of Parker and Ginobili, two future NBA stars, into the team's starting lineup. But Spurs' coach Gregg Popovich credited the example David had set for the entire team after Duncan was drafted. "[When] Timmy came along, David understood his talent and made it very easy for Tim to become the go-to guy. As Tim got older, he understood the value of Manu and Tony and was able to share that spotlight with them. I never had a talk. I never had a discussion, a meeting, or anything with any of those guys about that. We just did it."

Numerous NBA teams before and since have suffered through difficult transitions and "rebuilding" years, or have been torn apart by conflict between "stars" competing to be their team's leader. Popovich says the Spurs experienced no such turmoil or tension. "I [was] very fortunate I didn't have to deal with [our] stars' egos. I dealt with grown-ups who had character and prioritization already set in their lives and their values. It was because of their character we were able to do it." Indeed, the Spurs not only survived the transition, but also maintained a level of excellence from which they were poised to pursue and even achieve more and greater success.

While appreciating the recognition he received from his coach and his teammates for the leadership he displayed, David characteristically downplayed the credit. "I didn't necessarily think I wasn't the best player on the team [when Tim joined the Spurs]. I still felt like I had my own role to play. It's sort of like being a husband and a wife: Who's more important? Nobody's more important. You've both got your roles; you play your roles. And everything goes great as long as you play your roles. As soon as one of you guys acts like you run the show, and you're more important than the other one, everything goes haywire.

"I felt like my role was critical for this team. Even as I got older I felt like, how I come into this locker room, how I keep these guys together, keep them focused, keep the pressure off Tim until Tim's ready to become a leader ... all those things I thought were real important. All the pieces, that's the only way they can come together."

In his final years, after Tim Duncan established himself as the Spurs' most dominant player, David accepted and encouraged even younger teammates to take on their own leadership roles. And the new guys quickly came to respect and appreciate the Admiral's role on the team.

An article in *Sports Illustrated* reported at the time, "When young Spurs such as Tony Parker and Manu Ginobili see film of the young Robinson, they watch in wide-eyed wonder as this giant in short shorts with wheels worthy of a point guard soars above the basket to snare rebounds, block shots, and finish fast breaks. 'That's David?' they ask. 'No center in the history of the game,' says San Antonio coach Gregg Popovich, 'did the athletic things that David did in his prime.' "

With so much young talent assembled around him, David didn't need to do as many of those impressive "athletic things" his coach talked about to make his final season the perfect ending to his long and impressive career.

Duncan became the first player since Michael Jordan to win back-to-back, regular season MVP awards. And Parker and Ginobili quickly began to come into their own.

And at the end of the year, David celebrated with his teammates as he closed out his 14-year career with a second NBA championship. David played a significant role in that win, with 13 points, 17 rebounds, and two blocked shots in the clincher against the New Jersey Nets, to the cheers of a delirious San Antonio crowd in the rocking new SBC Center.

There could not have been a more befitting or memorable final game for David's memorable NBA career, which he ended as one of a dozen players in league history to make the 20,000 point/10,000 rebound club. A ten-time NBA All-Star, David followed his 1990 NBA Rookie of the Year Award with the NBA's regular season MVP in 1995.

Not only had David led the league in scoring in 1994, but he was also the NBA's top rebounder in 1991 and led the NBA in blocked shots in 1992. David and Kareem Abdul-Jabbar are the only two players in NBA history to achieve that trifecta.

The attention and the accolades continued to pour in for David in the wake of the Spurs' championship season and his own retirement. *Sports Illustrated* magazine recognized his contribution to the game of basketball and his impact on the world of sports by naming David, along with his friend and fellow teammate Tim Duncan, as their 2003 Sportsmen of the Year.

"It's great that they put us together," Duncan told the *San Antonio Express-News*. "It's an honor to be included in something like this with Dave. He defines sportsmanship."

In announcing the award, Terry McDonnell, managing editor of *Sports Illustrated*, said, "The selection was based not only on [David's and Tim's] playing success, but also on the way they have carried themselves in the community. They could have won this simply by what they did on the court, but behind their athletic contributions, when you look at the language of what this [award] has stood for, it's also been about character and sportsmanship."

The cover of the year's final issue of *Sports Illustrated* featured a picture of the two friends and teammates. The magazine's main story of the week had this to say, "For the six years that Robinson and Duncan shared the frontcourt and the spotlight—culminating with a decisive 88–77 victory over the New Jersey Nets in Game 6 of the Finals six months ago—they brought their team stunning success with surpassing tranquility. The Spurs won seven of every 10 regular-season games, never finished below second in the Midwest Division, and claimed a pair of NBA titles. While other franchises plowed through [difficult periods] of dissension and it's-my-team lip-flapping, nary a word of jealousy between Robinson and Duncan ever became public if, indeed, any was uttered at all.

"The two towering, tough-minded Spurs enhanced that landscape by showing that achievement and citizenship are not mutually exclusive. It is for being twin pillars of both a championship team and a community that we have chosen David Robinson and Tim Duncan as *SI*'s 2003 Sportsmen of the Year."

Many people asked David what he planned to do for the rest of his life, now that his basketball career had ended. (He was only 38 years old.) He admitted he still didn't have any definite long term plans. But he did say he remained committed to seeing The Carver Academy continue to grow and provide a brighter educational future for the children of San Antonio's Eastside.

"I don't see how I can get away from some kind of ministry," he added. "God's made that a part of my life. I know he wants me to share the Gospel somehow. I'm not a preacher. I'm more of a teacher. Education has always been important to me. I would enjoy teaching Bible study. So I expect he'll want me to do something along those lines. Whether it will be inside or outside a church situation, I don't know."

David also said he believed that, "God has given me my short-term marching orders. It's to become as good a husband and father as I can and to make this school [The Carver Academy] work. I have the faith to carry it out. It's going to work."

"So right now I know I'm where God wants me to be," he says, "and I couldn't be happier. Two years from now, five years from now, I don't know where it will be. But when the time comes, he'll open doors and pave the way for me. He'll make it clear what he wants me to do. And I'll be happy to do it."

Chapter 19

Family Guy

Looking back, David admits he would be hard-pressed to name the single biggest highlight of his basketball career. But he says the "best moment" of that career came at the end—winning the NBA championship again in his very last game and having Valerie, David Jr., Corey, and Justin there to share that night with him.

"It was a [terrific] way to end that period of my life. I was still healthy and, with my faith, I felt like, *Man, there are all these wonderful places I can go now, and things I can do still for the Lord, and this was just Phase One.* It was a great moment!" David smiles at the memory.

It's not as if David turned his back and completely walked away from that part of his life, or from basketball. He couldn't, and he never will. His athletic legacy will follow him forever. Just as David still follows, supports, and continues to be a positive influence on his San Antonio Spurs.

David watched and rooted as his former team and teammates won San Antonio's third and fourth NBA championships at the end of the 2004–05 and 2006–07 seasons. Of all the teams in the league, only the Boston Celtics, the Los Angeles Lakers, and the Chicago Bulls have won more.

In the 22 years since David joined the team, San Antonio has made the NBA post-season playoffs every year but one. And after their 2011–12 season, the Spurs established the record for most consecutive 50-plus win seasons — thirteen.

Before David was drafted number one in 1987, there was talk about the Spurs leaving the city. But there is no chance of that today. "The term *franchise player* is overused," says former long-time team owner Red McCombs. "But I'm not sure there would be a franchise here [in San Antonio today] without David."

It wasn't just his home city that honored and appreciated David's contribution to the game. In 2009, he was enshrined in the Naismith Memorial Basketball Hall of Fame in Springfield, Massachusetts. Then in 2012, twenty-five years after his graduation from the Naval Academy, the NCAA recognized David for his accomplishments and contributions to society with its prestigious Silver Anniversary Award.

But perhaps the most meaningful recognition for David came during his final season before retirement.

The NBA renamed its monthly award given to an NBA player for outstanding charitable off-court efforts. Every winner of the NBA's Community Assist Award now receives the *David Robinson Plaque,* which bears the inscription ". . . following the standard set by NBA Legend David Robinson who improved the community piece by piece."

Of course, David himself continued his personal commitment to improving the community (and the world) in which he lived not only "piece by piece" but also "person by person." And David decided to invest much of the extra time and energy he suddenly had in the "persons" he loved most in life—his wife and their three sons.

The travel required by his NBA career had made David an absentee dad every other week or so for eight to nine months of the year. So he happily determined to make a fast transition to full-time father for his three young sons. They were growing up fast, and there were so many important life truths he wanted them to learn.

"My number one priority when I retired was just to be home and spend as much time with my boys as possible," David says. "To be able to finally tuck them in every night and take them to school every morning. Just figuring out how to be Dad and a husband under a whole different set of circumstances. It was nice to have a normal family schedule again."

But David also got to see and do a whole lot of things he'd never had the chance to experience when he was growing up. Or when he was a professional athlete always concerned about his physical health. Like taking family ski trips to the Rockies where his sons searched out the biggest jumps on the slopes while David battled in vain just to keep his snowboard safely underneath him.

The Robinson boys sampled a variety of sports as they grew up. But David was careful to let them pursue their own interests and never force them to follow in his footsteps. "The [boys] do everything," he acknowledges. "They're active, and they get to experience things that I never had the opportunity to do, and that's been fun for us." (For example, as a grade schooler, Corey won a surfing contest and competed in a junior triathlon one summer in Hawaii.) "They're fearless and I'm not," David confesses. "So that's another part of the fun."

Of course David, like most dads, has goals for his sons. "I want them to have lives that mean something. I want them to understand the big picture. I don't particularly care about financial success. Sure it would be nice to see your kids *doing well*, but it's even better to see them *doing good*" and making a positive difference in the world and in the lives of people around them. That important lesson David constantly and consistently tries to teach his boys through his own example.

As this book goes to press, David Jr. is beginning his second year of college at the University of Texas in Austin. Corey is playing his senior season of high school football. A gifted athlete like his father, he hadn't taken any sport very seriously until his last couple years of high school. But he quickly got the attention of college coaches as a fast, six-foot-four-inch, sticky-fingered receiver and has verbally committed to play college football at Notre Dame. Justin is also in high school, two years behind Corey, and has a while to consider his decision about college. But when the time comes, his father is going to tell him the same thing he said to his older brothers: "Don't think you need to pick a certain college to please me, or your mother. And don't even begin to think about the sports opportunities, coaches, or anything else until you make certain the school offers what you need and want in terms of a quality education in the fields you're interested in. Academics first."

In addition to the increase in family time, a more "normal" schedule without at least four months on the road every year has made it much easier for David and his family to attend worship and become more active and involved members of Oak Hills Church in San Antonio. In fact, soon after retirement David began leading a men's Bible study that quickly began drawing more than 200 men every week.

But David has devoted a chunk of his time and energy in retirement to the The Carver Academy. He and Valerie eventually contributed over $10 million of their own money to launch and support TCA. But building a school from the ground up costs more than money. So after retirement, David often spent several days a week in his office at the school, working to raise millions more to help cover tuition for the majority of students at the school who were on scholarships.

"Watching the school grow, and watching children grow was one of the great joys of my life," he says. "[We] want to produce the next great generation of leaders."

In 2012, The Carver Academy became a public charter school affiliated with IDEA Charter Schools. The mission of this established, innovative, and growing network (more than 20 Texas schools already) is to prepare students from underserved, disadvantaged communities for success in college and citizenship.

"I'm excited about it," David told news reporters. "It's a win-win situation." He remained on the Carver board, and the school's name was changed to IDEA Carver Academy at the beginning of the August 2012 school year.

Chapter 20

Not Just Sayin'

"I've never been the kind of person who could sit still," David says. Which may partially explain why he started a whole new career that he hoped would create additional financial resources he could use to provide tuition scholarships for more Carver students.

The Admiral Center is an organization that partners with major corporations to help celebrities—from big-name athletes to famous entertainers—give their money to support significant projects that will not only benefit people and communities today, but will continue making an impact long into the future. The Center's clients include entertainment executives, musicians, actors, and NBA superstars.

The success and growth of these new business ventures was what motivated David to go back to school in 2010 to spend 18 months studying to earn a Masters in administration. Now a business man, he wanted to better understand the principles that enable companies and organizations to succeed. He also wanted to demonstrate to his sons and the students at TCA that learning is worthwhile and important at any stage of life.

To earn his degree and set an example, David studied 10 to 15 hours a week, turned all his work in on time no matter how busy he was or what else was going on in his life, and ended up graduating with distinction and a perfect 4.0 grade point average.

"It was tough," David says. "I'm not going to lie. I usually started my studying around midnight, after everyone else went to bed and [the house] was quiet. I had a lot at stake. I was running a school and had three kids of my own *in* school (one in college, two in high school)." Which was why he determined early on, "I'd better get all A's." And he did.

After all that he has achieved in life and all the success he has experienced, what would motivate a guy like David Robinson to not only pursue more education for himself, but also to passionately promote the importance of education to young people?

"After all my traveling in the NBA," David explains, "and seeing young kids in different cities and their priorities, it seemed like [things were] so skewed. Everybody wanted to be a rapper or a basketball player. And I just thought, *We need to address that basic flaw in our society and give kids an opportunity to see how great education is.* Once they do," he says, "all the limitations just start to disappear. And the future is unlimited!"

Andrew D. Bernstein/NBAE via Getty Images

David Robinson poses for a picture near a model ship called 'The Admiral' during the dedication of the Spurs Reading and Learning Center at Carver Academy in San Antonio, Texas.

David is also motivated by gratitude and the realization that he has been tremendously blessed. "I've been given ridiculous favor. When you're in a position of influence, with access, you can be a voice. I like to say, 'If you have a strong voice, don't whisper.'"

David certainly doesn't whisper. He uses his voice and the platform God has given him to preach and teach important messages to a broad audience of people. The importance and value of education is just one of those invaluable life messages. Another that is dear to his heart is the importance of giving.

David continues to be recognized and to receive prestigious awards for his philanthropy. But he doesn't do what he does for praise or plaques with his name engraved on them. When asked to explain his reasons, he tells a story.

David says he will never forget that moment in Madison Square Garden after the Spurs knocked off the New York Knicks in the finals of the 1999 playoffs and he lofted that first NBA championship trophy high over his head. It was gratifying. It was fulfilling. But it was nothing like giving to others.

"Winning a championship is so temporary," David says. "It's fantastic for the moment; don't get me wrong. You climb the hill. There's no greater feeling than standing there on the podium. But eventually, there's another hill to climb. It's fleeting glory, but intense.

"Giving is solid. It lasts a lifetime. You become linked with others. It's something that lasts forever. To be blessed enough to have something to give is unreal. It's amazing to me that God has entrusted me with this.

"Some worldly people say, oh well, it's only a small percentage of my income. But it's not just giving money. It's giving everything you have. The most important thing is giving [to others] who you are.

"I think giving back is so important for me ... because it's investing in the next generation. It's leaving your parts around so that you can be a part of the future. Who wouldn't want to give back? Who wouldn't want to build and see this tremendous monument or whatever that you've built; that you've been a part of that will impact generations to come. If I can build into the life of a young kid, or a young family, I'm a part of their life forever. I'm a part of this community forever.

"It's exciting to me that little bits of me will carry on the same way George Washington Carver still carries on today.

"I'll often go out and I'll quote him. I'll remind people that this man invented 250 uses for the peanut, 250 uses for the sweet potato. He transformed our lives, and we should be inspired by his attitude, inspired by his accomplishments. There's no excuse for us to sit on our laurels if this guy who had nothing could accomplish what he accomplished. He lives on in me, and I want to live on in the next generation."

Part of what David hopes will live on in the next generation are some of the many life lessons he's learned and regularly shares with others. For example, he says, "It's important to talk about forgiveness. We all need it. Everyone makes mistakes. But we also need to understand the dangers of sin. I know it's not popular to talk about sin today. Yet God tells us in the Bible that he wants us as his followers to be righteous. 'Be holy, because I am holy' (1 Peter 1:16). That's what we're supposed to do if we want to follow Christ. And those are incredibly high standards.

"That's what I try to tell kids. We can't be sucked into

what the world is trying to teach us. Through television we see all these marriages that really stink, and you see in real life that so many families are splitting up. But with God's help, you can have the kind of marriage he intended: you can love your spouse.

"People laugh and say 'Everyone cheats on his income tax.' But with God's help, you can live with integrity. It shouldn't matter what everyone else does.

"We as Christians need to take a stand for higher standards. All it takes is one little light, one candle in a pitch-black room, to make all the darkness go away. As a Christian, you can be that light. If you light one match, you can find your way around the room. And you can help those who will follow you find their way as well. Kids, and adults as well, need to realize God will show them the way. And he'll help them follow it."

David used to say that he felt he was more of a teacher than a preacher. These days he uses the loud voice he's been given to do a lot of both. But it's his actions, his example, the way he's lived and continues to live that shouts loudest of all.

"It's a bit glib to say that someone could be anything he wants to be," says Henry Cisneros, the former mayor of San Antonio whose office helped organize the extravagant, city-wide effort to welcome, host, and help recruit David for the Spurs after the team made him the number one selection in the 1987 NBA draft. "But it is absolutely the case with David. I've met every president since Jimmy Carter, as well as most of the men who ran for president, and David has the kind of qualities, the personal magnetism, the charisma, the intelligence to be presidential timber."

The Admiral has always been a leader. But what makes him most admiral-able, and the most crucial lesson he tries to convey to others, is this: As important and valuable as it is to use your gifts, your experience, and your voice to be a leader, it's even more important to be a follower—of Jesus.

Even as a follower, it's hard for a man who is seven-feet, one-inch tall to not stand out. But what really stands out about David Robinson is the way he uses all the physical stature he's been given and all the stature that he's earned throughout his life to lead and show others *the way, the truth, and the life*, so they too might become followers of Jesus.

David's Personal Testimony and Challenge to Readers

You are beginning your own legacy right now. What are people going to remember you for?

I want to encourage you in three things:

First—read and study your Bible so that you can understand the wisdom and truth found in there. What you learn will last you the rest of your life, it will guide you, it will protect you. It will be a lamp onto your feet and a light unto your path.

Second—pray. Prayer may be your greatest act of service. So pray every day. Your strength will be multiplied if you do. And it will prepare your heart to do the things necessary to help others.

Third—serve. Be a servant in all things in every situation—whether it's in your school work or your friendships. Whatever you do, think about doing it to serve the Lord. And then do it with a heart of service.

I was a basketball player. You wouldn't think anything good would come out of that, but God really used that opportunity to encourage many, many people.

I took my role very seriously. As I walked into the locker room every day, every year, I would say, "God, what would you like me to say in this locker room today? Who do you want me to encourage? What is the message you want me to give?" As Christians I believe that is how we should all approach life. Understand that whatever job you have, whatever setting you find yourself in is an opportunity the Lord gives you.

In the Bible, Joseph went to prison, but as he did he said, "Lord, what do you want me to do in here?" His whole heart was set for service, and God used him in a mighty way to save the national of Egypt and then to save his own family.

If you follow Joseph's example, if you make these three habits a daily part of your life, nothing will stand in your way. God will use you to accomplish great things.

Heart of a Champion: The Dominique Dawes Story

Kim Washburn

Her determination, dedication, and desire brought home the gold. Dominique Dawes focused on her dream, and nothing would stop her from reaching it—definitely not the fact that she was still just a kid. By the time she was fifteen years old, she stood on the podium to receive the Olympic gold medal in gymnastics. Discover how her faith in God and hard work led her to become one of

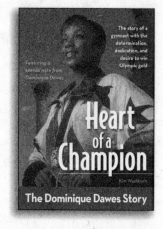

the top gymnasts in the world. Let her story and her motto of "determination, dedication, and desire" encourage you to become all you can be, in competition and in life. Includes a special note from Dominique Dawes.

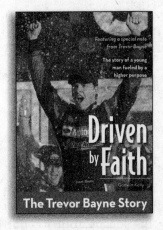

Defender of Faith: The Mike Fisher Story

Kim Washburn

Mike Fisher knows the true meaning of a power play.

As a veteran of the National Hockey League, Mike Fisher has a lot to be proud of. He plays for the Nashville Predators, was an alternate captain for the Ottawa Senators, competed in the Stanley Cup finals, and has been nominated for the Selke Trophy as the best defensive forward in the league. But it's not just his guts, grit, and talent that have brought him success. His power comes from the top—he puts his faith in Christ first and has demonstrated his love for God both on and off the ice.

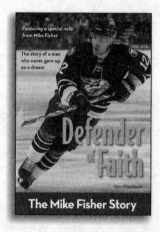

Includes a personal note from Mike Fisher.

Available in stores and online!

Toward the Goal: The Kaká Story

Jeremy V. Jones

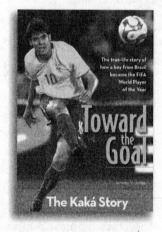

"I learned that it is faith that decides whether something will happen or not."

At the age of eight, Kaká already knew what he wanted in life: to play soccer and only soccer. He started playing in front of his friends and family, but when he suffered a crippling injury, doctors told him he would never play again. Through faith and perseverance Kaká recovered, and today he plays in front of thousands of fans every year. As the 2007 FIFA World Player of the Year and winner of the Ballon d'Or, this midfielder for Real Madrid has become one of the most recognized faces on the soccer field.

Available in stores and online!

Breaking Through By Grace: The Bono Story

Kim Washburn

When love walks in the room ...

Awards, fame, wealth ... Bono has it all. But the biggest rock star in the world has something more important, something that has guided every step of his success: faith in God. From growing up in Ireland during deadly times to performing on the largest stages in the world, Bono's beliefs have kept him grounded and focused on what truly matters. Whether using his voice to captivate an audience or to fight for justice and healing in Africa, Bono is a champion of the lost and a hero to those who long for harmony.

Gift of Peace: The Jimmy Carter Story

Elizabeth Raum

When Jimmy Carter was a boy, he listened to his parents talk about local politics and watched them live out their Baptist faith in the community. From the fields of his family farm to traveling the world negotiating peace talks, God guides every step of Jimmy's journey. His unwavering devotion to peace and faith helped him navigate the political waters of the governorship and presidency. Discover the extraordinary life of this world-famous humanitarian and follow in the footsteps of this incredible man of God.

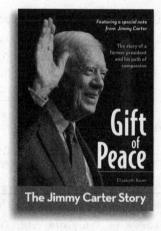

Available in stores and online!

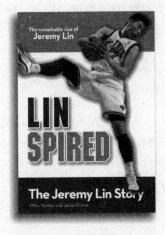

We want to hear from you. Please send your comments about this
book to us in care of zreview@zondervan.com. Thank you.

ZONDERVAN.com/
AUTHORTRACKER
follow your favorite authors